CONNECT THE DOTS

4 Habits of Mental Fitness to Think Clearly, Adapt, and Thrive

Dr.Derek Cabrera and Dr.Laura Cabrera

Odyssean Press cabreralab.org

Print ISBN: 978-0-9963493-5-2

To our children and grandchildren,

and to all the children of the world

who will one day grow into adults—

adults who will either build the world or break it.

This book is not written for children,

but it is written because of them.

Because when the work of mental development isn't done early,

it must be done later.

And too often, it's not done at all.

We live in a world shaped by adults—

many of whom were never taught to think clearly,

to manage complexity,

to regulate emotions,

to adapt with grace.

So this book is for the thinkers we can still become.

For the mental fitness we can still build.

For the second chances we must take seriously—

before we run out of time to connect the dots.

Table of Contents

Chapter 1: Why You Don't Have Time *NOT* to Think

There are two correlates I've come to see as undeniable truths—truths that thread through the fabric of every broken institution, fractured relationship, and social ill we face:

1. Unprepared adults raise unprepared children.

2. Hurt people hurt people.

Let that sink in. These aren't just sayings—they're systemic realities. They reverberate across time and space, across families and classrooms, across political aisles and boardroom tables.

And yet, we persist in a culture where we put nearly all of our resources into reacting to consequences rather than building capacity. Our schools, with the very best intentions—and the lagging support of outdated paradigms and underfunded systems—aren't producing prepared adults. Our parenting scripts, written by a perceived lack of time and frankly a fair bit of laziness and misinformation about human nature, often fail to adapt to today's complexities. And when adults make it to adulthood unprepared, it's not just a personal problem. It's a societal problem.

It's bad for business. It's bad for families.
It's bad for democracy. It's bad for mental health.
It's bad for the economy.

It's even bad for dating and finding love.

When people don't know how to think clearly, how to make meaning, how to organize information in ways that lead to understanding, empathy, or insight—then what you get is confusion, conflict, burnout, polarization, and pain.

In other words, unprepared minds produce unfit societies.

But here's the hopeful part: we can turn this around.

Mental fitness isn't magic—it's muscle. It's built through practice. And it's built around four simple, profound, universal patterns that underlie every act of thinking: Distinctions, Systems, Relationships, and Perspectives—DSRP. Together with the 6 Moves you'll learn in this book, DSRP forms the basis of the most powerful operating system your brain can run.

This book offers a way to train your mind the way we train our bodies—intentionally, consistently, and with purpose. It's not about intelligence. It's about practice. And practice leads to fitness.

You may think you don't have time to think.

But I promise you: you don't have time *not* to.

You may think thinking is a chore, a luxury, something reserved for academics and philosophers. But if you abdicate your responsibility to think for yourself, there's no shortage of industries ready to do it for you. The sugar industry. The fast fashion industry. The food industry. Social media algorithms. The "news" industrial complex. Politicians. AI. They are all more than happy to capitalize on your lack of mental fitness.

They don't mind doing your thinking for you. In fact, they prefer it that way.

But we don't.

And if you've picked up this book, I suspect you don't either.

What you hold in your hands is the toolkit for mental sovereignty—for reclaiming your most powerful human birthright: the ability to think clearly, compassionately, and systemically.

Backed by science.

Built for life.

Designed to scale—from schools to families to boardrooms to nations.

This book is a workout plan for the mind. It is also a call to action—for a mental fitness revolution. A revolution that starts not in some far-off capital, but right here: in your own head. In your family. In your community.

Because when we raise prepared minds, we raise prepared children.

When we strengthen minds, we heal people.

And when we connect the dots, we see the whole.

Let's begin.

Chapter 2: It's the Web, Not the Root

"We tried that, and it didn't work."
Are you sure?
Or did you just try one thread in a tangled web?

We live in a world that trains us to think in straight lines. If there's an effect, we want to trace it back to a cause. And if there's a problem, we want to solve it—fast. That sounds logical, responsible, even noble.

But in practice, this way of thinking fails us. Not because the world is too complex, but because we're using the wrong mental models to make sense of it.

Let's take a closer look.

One Cause, One Fix

This is where most of us begin: we see a problem and immediately look for the cause. Singular. Clean. Linear.

- The product isn't selling? Must be the marketing.
- The team is burned out? Must be poor time management.
- The country's divided? Must be social media.

This kind of *one-cause thinking* is deeply embedded in how we work, lead, vote, parent—even how we relate to our own sleep, diet, and health.

But here's the problem: *it's almost never true.*

"Root Cause" Thinking: A Slight Improvement

Somewhere along the way, we got a little more sophisticated. Instead of looking for just one cause, we now try to find the *root cause*. This approach asks "Why?"— then asks "Why?" again. And again. Until we get to the bottom of the issue.

It's often called the 5 Whys or root cause analysis, and it can be useful—especially in mechanical systems, like engines or machines, where failure is typically traceable to one component.

But here's the rub: people aren't machines. Organizations aren't engines. And real-world problems, like real world trees, rarely have just one root.

They have *roots*—plural. Twisted. Intertwined. Alive.

They have webs of causality.

The Reality: Webs of Causality

Most outcomes—good or bad—don't come from one cause. They emerge from interacting networks of conditions. They are produced not by one thing, or even one chain of things, but by a system of things.

The reason your product isn't selling may involve marketing, yes. But also timing. Market fit. Team morale. A pricing model that was copied from a competitor. Or a leadership assumption that went unquestioned for too long. All simultaneously contributing to the result.

That's what a web of causality is: A network of causes that are interactive, dynamic, and often simultaneous. They don't wait their turn. They don't act in isolation. They work together, in compounding and emergent ways. The effect is collective.

Why This Matters for You

- If you treat a web of causes like a row of dominoes, you'll misdiagnose.

- If you treat it like a tangled net, but only cut one string, the net stays tangled.

- If you attempt solutions one at a time, the web resists you.

- This is the trap of linear problem-solving.

- It leads to solutions that "should've worked" but didn't.

- Initiatives that looked great on paper but fell flat.

- Firefighting that never ends—because we never stopped to find the spark.

Connect the Dots (Literally)

That's what this book is about.

To "connect the dots" is not just a clever metaphor. It's a serious skill.

- It means seeing the structure underneath what looks like chaos.
- It means identifying the parts of the web—and how they're

connected.

- It means understanding that causes interact, reinforce, and cancel each other.
- And it means knowing that a solution that works must match the complexity of the problem.

From BIG problems to everyday problems—polarization, school shootings, inflation, immigration, climate, weight loss, burnout, sleep, raising teens—aren't solvable by picking a pet cause and hoping it sticks. They require simultaneous, systemic solutions. Which means we have to see the system first.

A Word on "Failure"

This is why some of our best ideas fail. Not because the ideas are bad. But because we try to implement them in *isolation*. We reduce a complex situation to one component. We intervene on that one point. And when it doesn't "fix" the whole, we wrongly conclude that it wasn't a real cause. But in a web, causes don't act alone. The system responds as a whole—or not at all. Just like improving your sleep won't work if you only turn off your phone—but still drink caffeine, ignore stress, and stay up too late. *All of the conditions* are part of the web. They must be addressed *together*.

The Myth of Sudden Problems

We often act like problems appear out of nowhere.

- "Suddenly, we lost market share."
- "Suddenly, I'm exhausted."
- "Suddenly, the team is burnt out."
- "Suddenly, my kid is struggling."

But very few things happen suddenly. Most "problems" are just the final dot in a long sequence we didn't notice. Understanding the web of causality behind the outcome lets us see not only what's happening, but why it's happening—and how it might have been prevented.

Seeing the Web Is the First Move

This book teaches you how to *see* webs of causality—through **six cognitive moves** that help you:

- Draw clearer **Distinctions**
- Understand **Systems** as parts and wholes
- Map **Relationships** that drive change
- Take multiple **Perspectives**

The six moves we will teach you are your tools to unpack the web of causality beneath every challenge you face. And, we know they work. The science behind them is convincing. They work in classrooms and boardrooms. In relationships and routines. In parenting and politics. In every domain where outcomes matter and systems are at play.

We're Not Saying It's Easy

This way of thinking isn't harder—it's just **different**. It's not difficult because the ideas are complex. It's difficult because they require us to slow down. To let go of our favorite assumptions. To stop trying to be the fixer and start being the observer.

Why It Matters Now

If you're reading this book, you already sense that something is missing in the way people think about thinking. The old ways of solving problems aren't working. They're too linear. Too narrow. Too simplistic. You're here because you want to learn to think in a way that reflects how the world actually works—a world made of networks, not lines. Of interactions, not events. Of patterns, not points. If we don't learn to see the web, we'll keep solving the wrong problems—and wasting our limited time, energy, and resources on things that don't work. But when we learn to see it—even just a little—it changes everything.

Chapter 3: Dots.

The Bridges of Königsberg

Centuries ago, Swiss mathematician Leonhard Euler (pronounced "Oiler") revolutionized the way we think about connectivity and problem-solving. In the 18th century, the city of Königsberg (now Kaliningrad) was divided by a river with seven bridges connecting different landmasses. The townspeople wondered: Could someone walk through the city, crossing each bridge exactly once and returning to their starting point? It seemed like a simple puzzle, but no one could find a solution—until Euler stepped in.

Rather than focusing on the city's geography, Euler simplified the problem into a network of dots and connections—what we now call graph theory. He represented land masses as "vertices" (dots) and the bridges as "edges" (lines connecting them). Through this abstraction, he discovered a fundamental principle: for such a path to be possible, each landmass must connect to an even number of bridges. Since Königsberg's layout didn't meet this condition, he proved that the walk was impossible.

Euler's insight laid the foundation for modern network theory, which underpins everything from social media algorithms and internet mapping to artificial intelligence and logistics. His breakthrough not only solved a centuries-old riddle but also transformed how we analyze connections and relationships in complex systems—a principle that still shapes the world today. When was the last time a mathematician rocked your world? You might be more connected to Euler than you think!

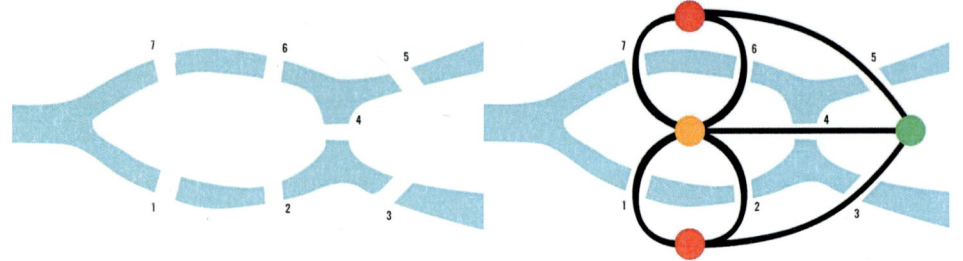

What Euler Got Right

It's downright impressive how such a simple mental abstraction ("dots" and "connections" or what network theorists call "nodes" and "edges") describes so much about the real world we live in. Euler's solution laid the groundwork for understanding complex networks in a simple, visual way. His insight allows us to map and analyze social networks, transportation systems, even neural pathways in the brain. In fact, the simple structural abstraction Euler discovered has led to modern AI and stands at the bleeding edge of nearly every field of science. The dots and lines he conceptualized are the foundation of how your social media feed is organized, how utilities distribute electricity and much more. You might even say that understanding networks is a superpower in the modern age. And it all starts with **dots** and connections.

Consider the internet—a vast network of networks. Data travels through nodes (dots) and links (connections), much like the bridges and land masses in Königsberg. Social media platforms use network theory to analyze and predict user behavior, connecting people across the globe. In healthcare, network theory helps map the spread of diseases, allowing for better prevention and treatment strategies. In neuroscience, it aids in understanding how neurons connect and communicate, unlocking secrets of the human brain. In fact, the very way we organize information to make meaning by creating mental models (M) is the result of how we organize (O) Information (I). When we look at multiple kinds of information through the lens of network structure we see that the simple structure of dots and connections is universal to all of them and characterizes how they are organized in reality.

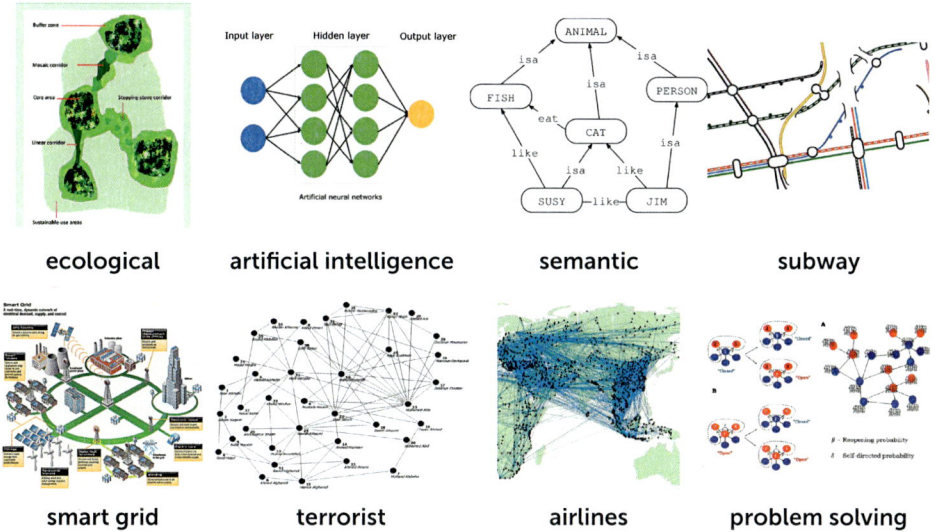

ecological	artificial intelligence	semantic	subway
smart grid	terrorist	airlines	problem solving

Whether analyzing terrorist networks, smart electricity grids, ecological systems, artificial intelligence processes, language structures, subway routes, airline operations, or collaborative problem-solving groups, the same fundamental pattern emerges: dots and connections. These seemingly different systems all share an underlying network structure, where nodes (dots) represent individual elements and edges (connections) define their relationships. This universal framework allows us to map, analyze, and optimize complex interactions across diverse fields.

So, from Euler we get a simple take away: **Connect the Dots.**

Activity:

Think about what matters to you (family, dog, job), what problems you're having (getting in shape, getting a better job, being more appreciative), what you're worried about (bills, teenagers, the economy, polarization), and simply connect the dots.

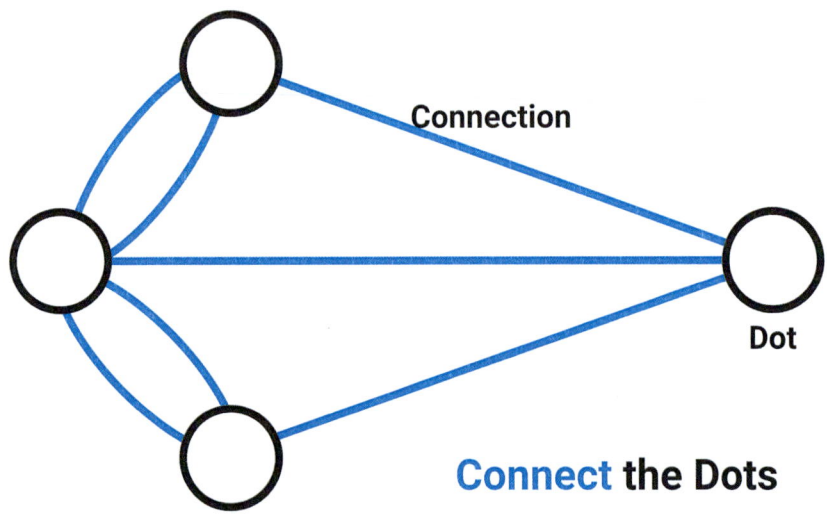

Connection

Dot

Connect the Dots

What Euler Missed

Euler's insight was groundbreaking, fundamentally shaping our understanding of networks for the past three centuries. However, just as astonishing as what he discovered is what he overlooked. While his findings have been a superpower for centuries, recognizing what he missed could be just as transformative for the future. Now, let's explore the hidden piece of the puzzle—what Euler didn't see and how his initial breakthrough has, ironically, kept us from seeing it for nearly 300 years.

- Every dot is a whole world in and of itself, containing networks of dots and connections inside it. Think about it: each land mass in Königsberg wasn't just a point on a map—it was a complex landscape with streets, buildings, people, and countless interactions. Each "dot" could be zoomed into, revealing another network of dots and connections.

- Every connection—the bridges—was its own form of "dot." The bridges themselves could be examined more closely, revealing materials, engineering designs, and the human efforts that built them. Each bridge is a collection of smaller dots and connections—planks, bolts, and supports—that together form a pathway. Each bridge isn't merely defined by what it connects, but is also a bridge, in and of itself. We could for example– using a large helicopter–come and remove the bridge and fly it to a parking lot.

- Various dots and connections could group together to form clusters distinctly different from other clusters. In social networks, for example, communities or friend groups form tight-knit clusters within the larger network. These clusters have unique properties and behaviors not apparent when looking at individual dots or the entire network.

- Every dot in the entire network is defined not only by what it is but also by "not being" all the other dots in the network. This concept of distinction is crucial; understanding what something is not helps define what it is. Each node gains identity through its relationships and differences with other nodes.

- Every dot—including every connection—is a unique point of view from which the network (in part or whole) can be seen. Each node has its own perspective, its own information about the network. The network looks different depending on where you're standing within it. This also means that the dots from which observation occurs are also part of the view from other dots' observations.

All of this provides invaluable insight into how our brain organizes information, using a fundamental structure of dots, connections, and hidden layers—what we call the DSRP framework: Distinctions, Systems, Relationships, and Perspectives. DSRP is the blueprint we use to make sense of the world, shaping the way we build and refine our mental models.

Chapter 4: Love Reality

"You don't see the world as it is.
You see the world as *you are*."
— Anaïs Nin (and every cognitive scientist, ever)

Reality doesn't need you to believe in it. It keeps doing what it's doing—with or without your opinion. And yet, most of what we suffer in life—at work, at home, in society—isn't due to reality itself, but to our resistance to it.

We argue with it.
We ignore it.
We manipulate it.
We cherry-pick it.
We fear it.

And do you know what reality does? It just keeps loving us back.

It keeps giving us feedback. It is the most patient, persistent, and stalwart teacher. Even when we ignore it, it keeps offering the lesson. No matter how many times we need to repeat, no matter how remedial we are, *reality is patient*. And it will always teach it to us again... and again... and again.

What can we do about it?
Recognize a powerful and invisible force: *Mental models*.

Mental Models: The Lens You Can't See

Every person on Earth is walking around with a mental model of how things work. Of how the world works. Of how *they* work. But here's the kicker: Most people don't know they have one. And if they do, they rarely stop to ask: *"Does it match reality?"*

That's the heart of what we call the **Reality Bias**—the #1 most dominant, dangerous, and universal bias we humans have. It's the tendency to believe that *our* perception of reality **is** reality. It's not. Our mental models are never perfect. At best, they're an approximation. A map—not the terrain. The more accurate our map, the more effectively we can navigate the world. The more distorted our map, the more we crash into the furniture of reality.

M = IO: How We Build the World in Our Heads

Let's break it down.

Your **Mental Model** (M) = how you **Organize** (O) **Information** (I).

$$M = I\,O$$

Every thought, decision, belief, or strategy you have is the result of how your brain has taken in information and organized it into a model of how things work. And that process of organization? It follows four universal rules. Four patterns found in everything from science to art to engineering to relationships.

Those patterns are:

- **Distinctions** (**D**): What something *is* and *is not*
- **Systems** (**S**): What *parts* something has, and what *whole* it's a part of
- **Relationships** (**R**): How things *interact* and affect one another
- **Perspectives** (**P**): The *point* and *view* from which something is seen

That's **DSRP**. And that's your O. Organizing information using DSRP is how you construct your mental model.

If DSRP is universal—why does it seem so hard? Because doing it well requires effort. Awareness. Practice.

We all make distinctions. But are they accurate, valid, or reliable?
We all see systems. But do we zoom in? Zoom out?
We all experience relationships. But do we map them? Name them?
We all have perspectives. But do we see them or seek others?

You don't get to choose whether you use DSRP and more than you get to choose whether to be impacted by gravity. What you get to choose is whether you are aware of it and use it to "Love Reality."

That's what **mental fitness** is: the capacity to use DSRP *on purpose*—with clarity, curiosity, and compassion.

And the best way to build that mental fitness?
Practice the **six Moves**.

These are the real-world exercises that develop each of the DSRP patterns in your daily life. They're how you rewire your brain to better model reality—and update your thinking when reality changes.

The Second Bias: Confirmation Bias

If Reality Bias is the #1 cognitive trap, **Confirmation Bias** is a close second. It's the tendency to seek out and favor information that confirms what we already believe (our mental model)—while ignoring or dismissing anything that contradicts it. It's why conspiracy theories persist. It's why feedback feels threatening. It's why change is so hard. It's why we cling to bad ideas, toxic relationships, and flawed strategies. Here's the hard truth: *We love our mental models more than we love reality.* But we have to reverse that…

The Love Reality Loop

There are only two ways you can live:

1. You can fit **Reality (R)** to your **Mental Model (M)**
   (Delusion. Denial. Defense.)

2. Or you can fit your **Mental Model (M)** to **Reality (R)**
   (Growth. Clarity. Peace.)

Fit R to M = bias, burnout, and blind spots

Fit M to R = learning, adaptation, and success

That's the **Love Reality Loop**. It means you don't assume your current beliefs are true. You hold them lightly. You let the world inform you. You treat disconfirming evidence as a gift—not a threat. That's what it means to *love* reality: To prioritize truth over comfort. To follow the signal, not the ego. To update your map when the terrain changes.

Why It Matters

You can't change what you can't see.

Mental models are the lens through which you see everything—your work, your relationships, your future. If the lens is off, everything gets distorted.

- You'll keep solving the wrong problems.
- You'll keep seeing "them" as the enemy.
- You'll keep blaming the system, or yourself—or both.
- And you'll wonder why nothing changes.

But when you love reality more than your opinions— when you stop trying to force the world to match your model, and instead reshape your model to fit the world—something incredible happens:

- You begin to see clearly.
- You adapt faster.
- You suffer less.
- You connect more.
- You become…free.

Practice Is the Path

This book isn't just about ideas. It's about **training**. If you want to love reality, you must get fit enough to see it. And that means practicing the **Six Moves**:

- Is/Is Not List
- Zoom In
- Zoom Out

- Part-Party!
- RDS Barbell
- P-Circle

These Moves are how you *build* and *update* your mental models with DSRP. They are how you overcome the two greatest biases we face. They are how you learn to see clearly—so you can live wisely. *You cannot out-think reality.* But you can learn to think with it. And when you do, everything changes.

Now, let's practice.
Let's train.
Let's love reality.

Chapter 5: It's Not About the What, It's About the *HOW*

In this chapter we are going to quickly show you the deep scientific theory that underlies how your brain thinks–how it organizes information. There are remarkable benefits to understanding this theory in terms of complex abilities. However, after we show you the theory, we are going to make it much simpler to practice by learning six mental moves that research shows gets you most of the benefits.

Every thought you've ever had—every insight, every misunderstanding, every decision or discovery—has been shaped by an invisible structure. That structure is *DSRP-483*.

DSRP-483 is a simple yet profound framework that reveals how we think—beneath the content of what we think about. It stands for:

- **D**istinctions
- **S**ystems
- **R**elationships
- **P**erspectives

These four simple patterns, when practiced deliberately, give rise to clearer thinking, better problem-solving, more adaptive behavior, and deeper understanding. 4 Patterns, 8 Elements, 3 Dynamics. Let's break them down.

1. The Four Universal Patterns

These are the core structures that underlie all cognition:

Distinctions (D)

We understand things by making distinctions: what something **is** and what it **is not**. Identity is defined by contrast.

- **Elements:** Identity (i) and Other (o)
- **Every thought you have is about something—and not something else.**

Warm-Up Activity:

Pick an object near you (e.g., "coffee"). Fill in:

What It Is	What It Is Not
A brewed beverage	Not a soft drink
Contains caffeine	Not decaf (in this case)
Consumed hot or cold	Not solid

Systems (S)

Everything is a part of something and has parts itself. Our ability to zoom in and out gives context and precision.

- **Elements:** Part (p) and Whole (w)
- **We understand things by seeing their parts and wholes.**

Warm-Up Activity:

Pick a system (e.g., "Company") and complete:

Whole System	Parts
Company	Engineering, Sales, Marketing, HR, Legal

Now pick a *part* (e.g., "Sales") and Zoom In again:

Whole System	Parts
Sales	Sales Strategy, Lead Generation, Presales / Sales Enablement, Inbound Sales, Outbound Sales, Account Executives / Closers, Customer Success / Post-Sales, Sales Operations, Sales Leadershipl

Relationships (R)

Things do not exist in isolation. They affect and are affected by other things. Seeing these interactions helps us understand cause and effect.

- **Elements:** Action (a) and Reaction (r)

- **Every relationship is a two-way influence.**

Warm-Up Activity:

Choose two things that relate (e.g., "Rain" and "Plants"):

Action	Reaction
Rain provides water	Plants grow

Now try naming the relationship: *Hydration Cycle*

Perspectives (P)

Every observation is shaped by a point of view. Recognizing multiple perspectives helps us overcome bias and deepen understanding.

- **Elements:** Point (ṗ) and View (v)

- **Every perspective has a view from a specific point.**

Warm-Up Activity:

Topic: "Homework.":

Point (Who/What)	View (What they see)
Student	Stress, time pressure
Teacher	Practice, assessment tool
Parent	Responsibility, learning

Warm-Up Activity:

Topic: "implementing a new software system"

Point (Who/What)	View (What they see)
IT Manager	Technical integration, system compatibility, cybersecurity
Finance Lead	Budget allocation, ROI, cost-saving potential
End User (Employee)	Learning curve, workflow disruption, usability
HR	Training needs, change management, employee satisfaction
Executive Leadership	Strategic alignment, scalability, long-term impact
Customer	Improved service, potential for errors during transition
Cost (Conceptual)	Upfront investment, opportunity cost, long-term savings

2. The Eight Elements

Each of the four patterns is made up of two co-implicating elements—this means they always exist in pairs:

Pattern	Element 1	Element 2
Distinctions	identity (i)	other (o)
Systems	part (p)	whole (w)
Relationships	action (a)	reaction (r)
Perspectives	point (ṗ)	view (v)

You can't have one without the other. To define a concept (i), you're also implying what it is not (o). If you recognize a whole, you're implicitly identifying parts. This is the first of three powerful rules that govern how our thinking works.

3. The Three Dynamics

These are not extra rules—they're the deeper logic embedded in how thinking *moves*. They describe the *physics of thought*.

1. Elemental Co-implication (↔)

If you have one element, you necessarily have the other. They are co-implicative.

- identity ↔ other
- part ↔ whole
- action ↔ reaction
- point ↔ view

Warm-Up Activity: "If One Exists, the Other Must"

For each example, state something you know or observe (Element A), and then identify the co-implicative element (Element B) that must also exist—even if it isn't mentioned or noticed. This trains your mind to see the invisible structure beneath the information.

Pattern	Element A (Observed)	Element B (Implied)
Distinction	I see a tree.	There is a boundary between tree and not-tree (e.g., a bush, a rock).
System	This is a team member.	There must be a team (whole) that this person is part of.
Relationship	Giving feedback to a coworker.	There is a response (internal or external) to that feedback.
Perspective	A student shares their opinion.	That view comes from a point—their experience, background, or role.

Key Takeaway for Practice:

- When you hear a view, ask: *What's the point of that view?*
- When you define something, ask: *What is it not?*
- When you see a part, ask: *What is the whole it belongs to?*
- When you observe an action, ask: *What reaction might that cause (or come from)?*

This builds mental reflexes that help you spot structure in real time—making your thinking sharper, deeper, and far more complete.

2. Equality (=)

The four patterns of DSRP—Distinctions, Systems, Relationships, and Perspectives—are not defined by dictionary definitions of those words. They are defined structurally by what they *equal*.

Each pattern is the equality of its two co-implicative elements. That is:

- A Distinction *is not* simply "a difference between things."
  A Distinction is defined as: D = identity (i) and other (o)
  This means: whenever you define or identify something, you are also (by definition) excluding what it is not.

- A System *is not* just "a collection of parts."
  A System is defined as: S = parts (p) and whole (w)

To recognize a part is to imply a whole; to define a whole is to imply parts.

- A Relationship *is not* just "a connection between things."
  A Relationship is defined as: R = action (a) and reaction (r)
  Every cause has an effect; every interaction has two ends.

- A Perspective *is not* just "a viewpoint."
  A Perspective is defined as: P = point (ṗ) and view (v)
  A view is always seen from a point. A point always carries a view.

These equations are not metaphors. They are literal:

Each pattern equals its two structural elements.

That is the definition of the pattern.

If either element is missing or unclear, the pattern is incomplete.

Warm-Up Activity: Define the Pattern by Its Structure

Write the full structural equation for each pattern. This isn't memorization—it's about learning to *see structure in everything*.

Pattern	Equation	Structural Definition
Distinctions	$D = i \leftrightarrow o$	identity co-implies other
Systems	$S = p \leftrightarrow w$	parts co-implies whole
Relationships	$R = a \leftrightarrow r$	action co-implies reaction
Perspectives	$P = \dot{p} \leftrightarrow v$	point co-implies view

Bonus: Next time someone throws around the word "system," "relationship," or "perspective," ask yourself: *Can I see both elements?*

If not, the structure is incomplete—even if the vocabulary sounds right.

3. Simultaneity (*)

This is the most powerful and most often misunderstood rule:
Every concept is made up of all eight elements—simultaneously.

That means any idea, object, system, or problem *contains within it*:

- identity (i) and other (o)
- part (p) and whole (w)
- action (a) and reaction (r)
- point (ṗ) and view (v)

Not metaphorically—literally. If you *zoom in* on any "dot," all eight elements are embedded in it. That's what gives DSRP-483 its predictive power: when you examine a single idea, you can anticipate which elements are underdeveloped or missing. Every idea is a door to deeper structure.

Warm-Up Activity:

Pick any single concept (e.g., "Smartphone") and identify all 8 elements it contains:

Element	Your Example
smartphone as an identity (i)	A mobile device
smartphone as an other (o)	Not a landline / Not a laptop
smartphone as a part (p)	Part of digital ecosystem, app economy
smartphone as a whole (w)	Made up of parts: Screen, battery, software
smartphone as an action (a)	Sends messages
smartphone as a reaction (r)	[the set of actions that results in] the existence log a smartphone
point (ṗ)	Looking at something from the point of view of a smartphone
view (v)	Viewed by user, manufacturer, regulator; Seen as tool, toy, threat, or necessity

The Big Insight

When we realize that everything is already structured, we stop looking at information as flat. We see its depth. We begin to expect the 8 elements and inquire when they're missing. That's what gives DSRP-483 its real power: it turns cognition into a diagnostic and predictive tool.

You'll start spotting gaps:

- That argument lacks a "reaction."
- This plan doesn't have a "whole."
- That opinion ignores the "other."
- This idea is missing a "point of view."

And you'll fill them in. That's how you learn to think in 3D—fluidly, flexibly, systemically. That's how you connect the dots.

Why This Matters

When you practice DSRP-483, you're not just learning a theory. You're learning *how to think*—with structure, depth, and clarity. You're gaining cognitive agility in a world of complexity. You're also building the mental muscles to:

- Communicate more clearly
- Lead more effectively
- Learn faster
- Navigate ambiguity
- Solve complex problems

And most importantly—you're connecting the dots.

Chapter 6: Start with any Dot—and Dig Deeper

Think about your daily life. Each interaction, every piece of information you consume, each decision you make—they're all dots. But each of these dots contains its own network. Your morning coffee isn't just a beverage; it's connected to farmers who grew the beans, the supply chain that transported them, the barista who prepared it, and even the cultural rituals surrounding coffee.

The barista who hands you the coffee is another dot. But she is also a network of experiences, skills, relationships, and aspirations. She interacts with coworkers, has her own social circles, and contributes uniquely to each customer's day.

When we start to pay attention, we begin to see the lines that connect these dots—not just superficially but in depth. We realize that connecting the dots isn't just about drawing lines; it's about exploring the networks within each dot and understanding the multifaceted relationships between them.

Activity: Map Your World

Grab a pen. Sketch your family, job, or biggest problem as dots and connections. Then zoom in—what networks live inside each dot?

See Networks Within Networks

This is where modern network theory, enriched by the DSRP framework, comes into play. At its core, it's about understanding how individual elements are connected and how these connections shape the behavior of the whole system.

But with DSRP, we recognize that each element is also a system of its own, full of internal connections and perspectives.

Consider your social media networks—Facebook, Instagram, LinkedIn, Twitter (or X, as it's now known). Each friend or follower is a dot in your social network. But each person is also a complex system—an entire network of experiences, relationships, and thoughts. The interactions you have—the likes, comments, shares—are not just lines connecting dots; they're rich relationships influenced by perspectives, contexts, and distinctions.

Our economic system is another network of networks. The stock market isn't just dots and lines; each company is a system with its own internal networks of employees, products, and strategies. Banking networks like SWIFT, Visa, and Mastercard aren't just conduits for money; they are complex systems that affect global economies and individual lives.

When you hop on a plane, you're engaging with a transportation network. But each airplane is a system of systems—engines, navigation systems, crew members—all working together. Airlines like Delta and Emirates manage fleets, routes, customer service, and logistics, each a network within the larger transportation network.

Let's bring this closer to home. Think about your health. Healthcare and insurance networks, like Blue Cross Blue Shield and hospital systems, are the infrastructure that supports your well-being. But your own body is a network—a system of organs, cells, and biochemical processes. Each cell is a dot with its own functions and interactions.

Our environment operates on networks too. An ecosystem is a network of organisms and their physical environment, each component a system within itself. A single tree is a network of roots, branches, leaves, and the microorganisms that inhabit it.

Your education is a networked experience. Each subject you study is a system of concepts and ideas. University alumni networks and academic collaborations are clusters within the broader network of knowledge, each contributing unique perspectives and insights.

See the Bigger—and Smaller—Picture

So why does all this matter? Because recognizing these networks within networks—and our place within them—allows us to navigate life more intentionally. When we understand that every dot and every connection contains its own network, we become more aware of the depth and complexity of the world around us.

By seeing the DSRP structure that Euler overlooked, we can see how we create mental models. In other words, we understand *how we understand things*. We learn to make distinctions, clarifying what things are and what they are not, which enhances our understanding. We recognize systems, seeing how parts fit within wholes and how wholes are made up of interconnected parts. We identify relationships, understanding how elements influence and interact with one another. Finally, we adopt multiple perspectives, appreciating different viewpoints that foster empathy and lead to better decision-making. Together, these metacognitive abilities provide a deeper, more flexible way to process information, solve problems, and navigate complexity. We connect the dots. We see the bigger and smaller pictures.

Connecting the dots is more than a theoretical idea—it is a deeply personal and transformative way of understanding the world. It reveals how something as simple as your morning coffee links you to global trade networks, illustrating that every aspect of your life is both an individual dot and part of a vast, interconnected system. Each element influences and is influenced by countless others, forming a dynamic web of relationships that shape our daily experiences. By mapping these dots and their connections, and by uncovering the networks within each dot, we gain a deeper understanding of the complex systems that drive our world. Every decision we make extends beyond a simple connection between two points; instead, it engages with interwoven, multilayered systems, each structured by its own distinctions, relationships, and perspectives. Recognizing these deeper connections broadens our awareness, enabling us to navigate complexity with greater clarity, adaptability, and insight.

As we embark on this journey into networks within networks, I invite you to take an active role in connecting the dots of your own life. Pay attention to the nodes you encounter—the people, ideas, and experiences that shape your world—and consider how they interconnect, not just at the surface level but in the deeper, often unseen structures beneath. In the chapters ahead, we will uncover the hidden patterns that define our world, exploring how the DSRP framework can drive innovation, build resilience, and create meaningful change.

The beauty of a connect-the-dots puzzle isn't just in the final image—it lies in the process of discovery. Each dot represents a universe of possibilities, and each connection is a pathway to new insights. By embracing both Euler's groundbreaking insights and the unexplored potential of DSRP Theory, we gain a powerful tool for understanding and shaping the world around us.

Just as connecting the dots in a puzzle reveals a bigger picture, sharpening our ability to think systematically unlocks a deeper understanding of the world. But knowing how to connect the dots is only the beginning—true mastery comes from practicing the skills that make those connections stronger and more meaningful. Just like any learned ability, thinking is something that can be trained, refined, and improved with the right approach. This brings us to a powerful insight: a small, focused effort can lead to meaningful improvements in our ability to think, problem-solve, and navigate complexity. To see this in action, let's explore how deliberate practice transforms our ability to connect the dots effectively.

Chapter 7: Connect the Dots

Imagine stepping into your backyard with a javelin—a spear-like object you've never held before. In just an hour, you learn to grip it properly, position your body, and release it with a flick of your wrist. You might not be Olympic-ready, but here's the astonishing truth: you'd likely be better at throwing a javelin than 80% of the world's population. That's the power of even a small amount of focused practice—a concept deeply rooted in the Pareto Principle, also known as the 80/20 rule or the "Biggest Bang for Your Buck" principle.

Named after Italian economist Vilfredo Pareto, who observed that 80% of Italy's land was owned by 20% of the population, this principle extends to nearly every area of life. In business, 80% of sales often come from 20% of clients. In software, 80% of user complaints stem from just 20% of bugs. Even in personal development, small, targeted efforts often yield outsized improvements. The same applies to your thinking skills. The first few hours of learning something new, whether it's javelin throwing or mental exercises, create remarkable gains. But there's an even deeper insight—applying the 80/20 rule to itself. Not only is practice essential, but knowing what to practice makes all the difference. A great coach or a focused strategy helps you identify the most effective exercises, ensuring that your efforts build your fitness.

Train Your Mind Like You Train Your Body: The Future is Mental Fitness

Imagine a world where no gyms, no workout routines, and no personal trainers existed, and the only time you received help for your physical health was after an injury. There would be no guidance on how to build strength, improve endurance, or maintain flexibility—just hospitals and physical therapists waiting to step in when something went wrong. Absurd, right?

Yet, this is exactly how we treat mental fitness today. We expect our minds to perform at their best without training them. We wait until we feel overwhelmed, stuck, or burned out before seeking help. We rely on therapy and crisis management but lack the everyday mental "workouts" that keep our minds sharp, resilient, and adaptable.

Just as physical fitness strengthens your body, mental fitness strengthens your mind, making your thinking clearer, more agile, and more adaptive.

Mental Fitness is the ability to adapt and thrive in any situation or environment

Thinking isn't just something we do—it's our fundamental tool for adapting to life's ever-changing challenges. Unlike animals, who adapt primarily through physical means, humans uniquely thrive by altering their thinking. When you become mentally fit, you improve your ability to navigate uncertainty, complexity, and emotional stress with greater ease and effectiveness.

At the heart of mental fitness are mental models—the internal frameworks or beliefs that shape your perception of the world. These mental models are essentially your mindset, assumptions, beliefs, or biases; they define your understanding, guide your actions, and influence your emotions. By intentionally refining and challenging these mental models, you cultivate an adaptable, dynamic Mindflow—a constantly evolving mental state that allows you to effectively respond to any situation.

In essence, your mental models are your beliefs, assumptions, mindset, and perceptions. Improving your mental fitness means actively refining these models, empowering you to navigate life's complexities, communicate more effectively, make better decisions, and enhance your emotional intelligence. Just as physical exercise reshapes your body, mental exercises reshape your mind—enabling you to thrive in every aspect of your personal and professional life.

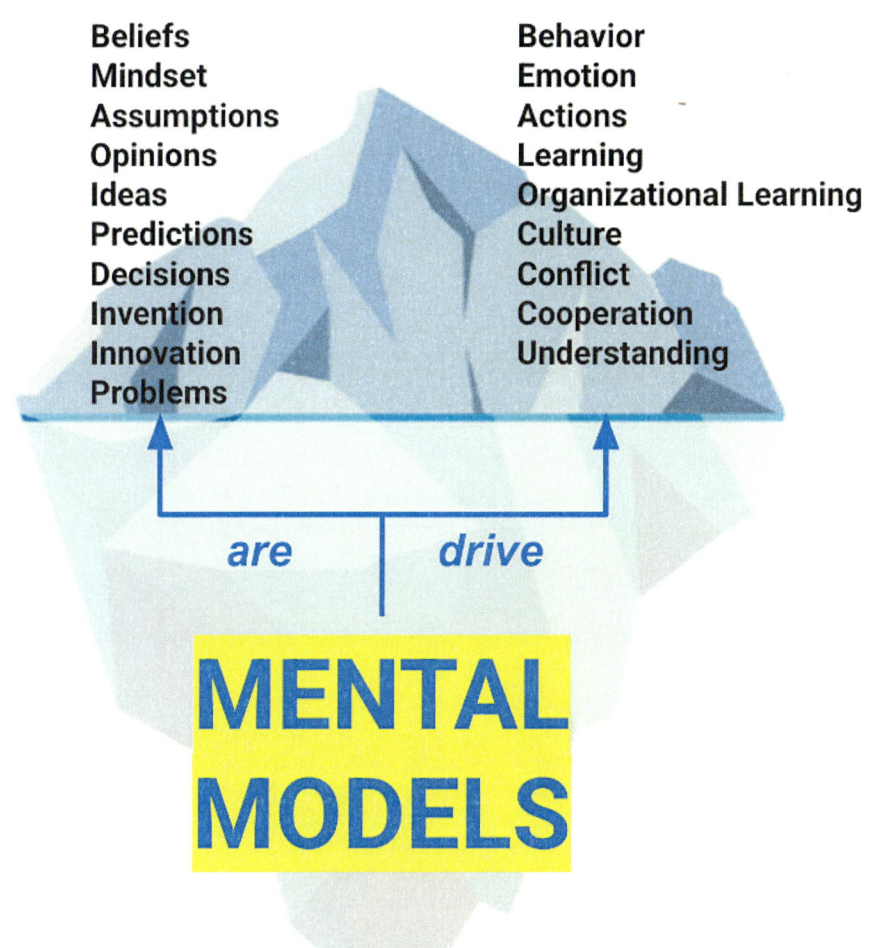

Beliefs
Mindset
Assumptions
Opinions
Ideas
Predictions
Decisions
Invention
Innovation
Problems

Behavior
Emotion
Actions
Learning
Organizational Learning
Culture
Conflict
Cooperation
Understanding

are   *drive*

MENTAL MODELS

At Cabrera Research Lab, we've spent 25 years studying how humans think—how we predict, behave, make decisions, and process the world around us. Just as sports scientists study the body to optimize physical performance, we've mapped out how the mind works so we can train it to function better. The next step? Applying this knowledge to create structured mental fitness training—the same way we've done for physical fitness.

We're not talking about brain games, puzzles, or meditation apps—they may provide temporary stimulation, but they lack real-world transfer. Functional fitness isn't about lifting random objects; it's about training movements that make you stronger in everyday life. Similarly, mental fitness should sharpen the skills that matter most—problem-solving, decision-making, creativity, and resilience.

A great physical workout improves strength, endurance, flexibility, and balance. A great mental workout enhances problem-solving, systems thinking, decision-making, introspection, and emotional intelligence.

Just like physical fitness, mental fitness needs intentional training—and once you start, the benefits compound over time. A strong mind is essential for every aspect of life. Whether you're a student, a parent, a leader, or a professional, mental fitness helps you:

1. Make better decisions, faster. Get to the root of problems, see patterns, and anticipate challenges.

2. Think more clearly and deeply. Cut through distractions and see complex ideas from multiple perspectives.

3. Adapt to change with confidence. Navigate uncertainty and complexity without feeling overwhelmed.

4. Communicate more effectively. Express ideas with clarity and understand others more deeply.

5. Strengthen emotional resilience. Handle stress, setbacks, and difficult situations with greater control.

Whether you're a parent navigating the challenges of raising a teenager, a student trying to grasp complex subjects, a scientist breaking new ground in research, a business leader making high-stakes decisions, a designer innovating new products, or a factory worker optimizing daily processes, the same core mental skills apply across every profession and stage of life.

Practicing these moves rewires your brain for better thinking—just like a workout routine squats builds physical endurance—so too can a mental fitness routine:

Step 1: Build Awareness – Start noticing how you think. Pay attention to the mental moves you already use, like making lists, comparing ideas, or structuring arguments.

Step 2: Practice the First 5 Moves – Choose one mental move each day and apply it deliberately. For example, when reading the news, practice seeing the distinctions, relationships, and perspectives at play.

Step 3: Track Your Progress – Just like logging workouts at the gym, track how these mental exercises improve your clarity, problem-solving, and decision-making over time.

Step 4: Make It a Habit – Repetition builds strength. The more you train these skills, the more automatic and powerful they become.

Step 5: Challenge Yourself – Just like increasing weights at the gym, push yourself to apply these mental moves in more complex situations—big decisions, strategic thinking, or creative problem-solving.

Many of us go through life on autopilot, overwhelmed by distractions and reacting rather than thinking proactively. The result? Poor decision-making, struggles with complex ideas, emotional overwhelm, stress, and missed opportunities. But it doesn't have to be that way. With the right training, you can unlock a sharper, more resilient, and more capable mind. Imagine waking up each day with greater clarity in decision-making, the ability to solve problems faster and more effectively, more confidence in tackling challenges, and a deeper understanding of yourself and the world.

The First Set

Research in cognitive science (see Appendix 1) reveals that the First Set of mental moves operate under the Pareto Principle for thinking—a small set of core skills that yield outsized results. Mastering these fundamental moves gives you a cognitive edge, allowing you to think faster, reason more effectively, and approach problems with greater creativity than most people. They are simple enough to practice daily, yet powerful enough to reshape the way you process information and make decisions.

With just a few minutes of practice each day over a couple of weeks, you'll see noticeable improvements in problem-solving, communication, decision-making, and creativity. These mental moves strengthen the foundations of clear and structured thinking, enabling you to tackle complex challenges, articulate ideas with precision, and generate innovative solutions with ease.

Think back to the javelin. The initial practice won't make you an Olympian, but it builds a foundation that sets you apart from most. Similarly, practicing the First Four mental moves won't make you a genius overnight, but it will make you more mentally fit than most people—and more adaptable (and therefore smarter) than any AI.

The key is repetition. Just as regular physical exercise strengthens your body, consistent practice of mental moves builds cognitive fitness. Over time, these moves become second nature, seamlessly integrating into your thinking process. Whether you're brainstorming at work, tackling challenges at home, or making quick decisions on the go, these cognitive tools will enhance your ability to analyze, adapt, and innovate effortlessly. The more you practice, the sharper and more automatic your thinking becomes.

The First Set of mental moves are foundational techniques that sharpen your ability to analyze, organize, and connect ideas. These include:

- Is/Is Not List: Clearly defining what something is and what it is not, refining focus and understanding.
- Zoom In/Zoom Out: Breaking down wholes into parts and recognizing how those parts fit into a larger system.
- Part-Party: Asking if the parts of a system are related.
- RDS Barbell: Identifying relationships and their components to see how elements influence one another.
- Perspective Circle: Viewing situations through multiple lenses, enhancing critical thinking and empathy.

Think of these moves as the push-ups and squats for your mind—simple, powerful, and endlessly versatile. Just as push-ups and pull-ups build strength and endurance, these mental exercises develop the skills necessary to solve problems, communicate clearly, and think adaptively. Without basic tools like lists and graphs, it would be difficult to process and organize information effectively. Mastering the First Set of moves extends this capability, providing a framework to navigate complexity with ease.

The journey to seeing more and connecting the dots starts with a single step. By committing just a few minutes a day to practicing these moves, you'll begin to see patterns and relationships where others see confusion. You'll gain clarity in decision-making, solve complex problems faster, and approach challenges with greater adaptability. Most importantly, you'll develop a mind that's sharp, flexible, and prepared for anything life throws your way. Now, let's dive into each of the First Four moves, complete with practical exercises to get you started.

Chapter 8: Is/IsNot List Move

Is/Is Not List Move

The story of Abraham Wald and the Missing Bullet Holes serves as a remarkable illustration of the power of distinctions, akin to the concept of **Is/ IsNot List**. In this tale, Wald's unconventional approach challenged the conventional wisdom of military officers tasked with protecting aircraft. Their initial assumption was to reinforce the areas on planes where bullet holes were most abundant, a logical but incomplete perspective.

Wald, armed with a different set of distinctions, saw beyond the obvious. He realized that the data they had was from planes that had survived their missions and returned, and it didn't account for the planes that didn't make it back. By making a critical distinction between the two groups, he arrived at a counterintuitive conclusion: the armor should be placed where the bullet holes were absent, particularly on the engines.

This shift in perspective encapsulates the essence of **Is/IsNot List** – the ability to make distinctions that challenge our assumptions and reveal hidden insights. In Wald's case, he didn't follow the path of least resistance; he questioned the assumptions of the military officers and dug deeper. He understood that the foundation of any decision, whether in the context of aircraft armor or any other field, lies in the distinctions we make. Wald's approach prompts us to look beyond the obvious, consider alternative viewpoints, and test our assumptions.

Is/IsNot List

The Is/IsNot List is a powerful tool for clarity, critical thinking, and decision-making. It sharpens our ability to make distinctions, allowing us to see what something is while simultaneously defining what it is not. This structured approach not only enhances understanding but also helps us uncover nuances and perspectives that might otherwise go unnoticed. By practicing this cognitive move, we strengthen our ability to think critically, make informed choices, and refine our conceptual understanding.

At its core, the Is/IsNot List works by distinguishing an identity (i) from its other (o). It prompts us to create two columns: one listing the defining characteristics of what something is, and the other listing what it is not.

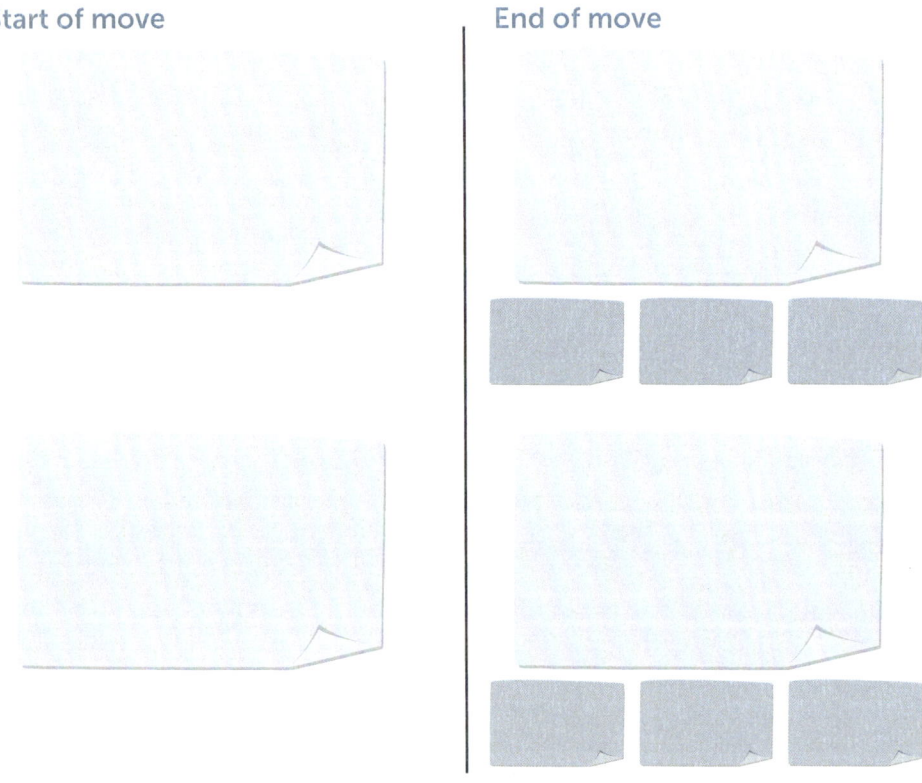

Start of move

End of move

This process clarifies boundaries, ensuring a deeper and more precise grasp of a concept. However, a common mistake is to list only parts of a thing rather than defining its essential nature. The Is/IsNot List requires explicit distinctions between what belongs to the identity and what does not, ensuring a more meaningful and accurate understanding.

This cognitive tool is invaluable in academics, problem-solving, and professional decision-making. Whether breaking down complex ideas, analyzing challenges, or seeking clarity in intricate projects, the Is/IsNot List provides a structured approach to understanding and differentiation. It illuminates hidden connections, helps navigate complexity, and fosters deeper insights.

As part of the DSRP framework, the Is/IsNot List serves as a cornerstone of structured thinking. By mastering this move, we develop a clearer, more precise mental framework, enabling us to navigate an increasingly complex world with confidence. As we continue exploring DSRP, embracing the Is/IsNot List will unlock new levels of clarity and understanding, making it an essential skill for anyone seeking to refine their thinking. Here are Is/IsNot Lists examples for each of the diverse concepts, ideas, or things mentioned earlier:

Examples
1. Communication: we can use Is/Is not List to answer the question, **"What is effective communication?"**

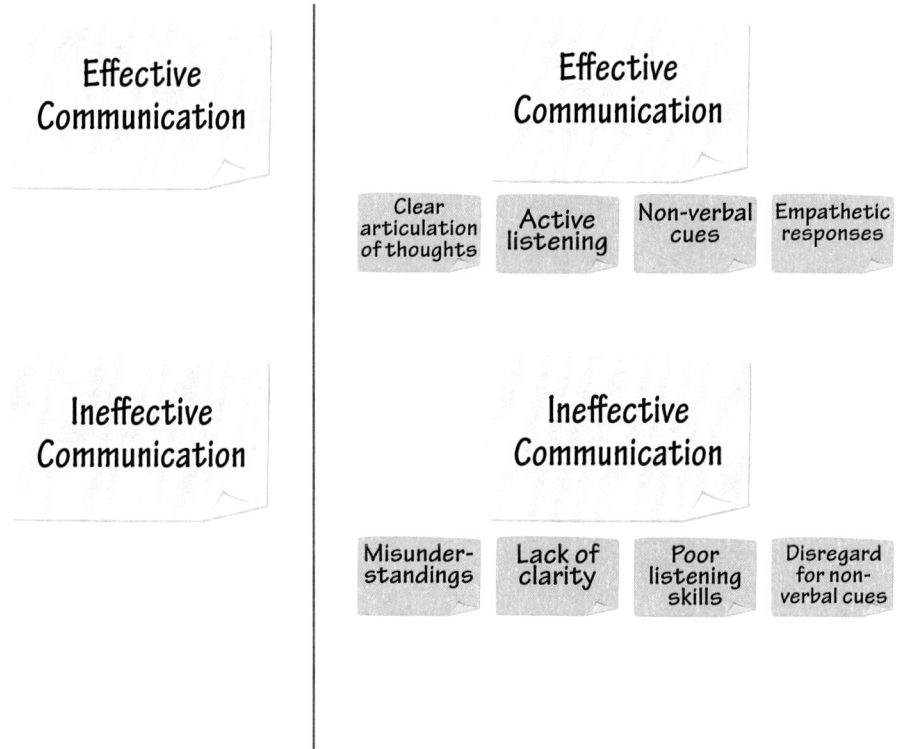

2. Leadership:

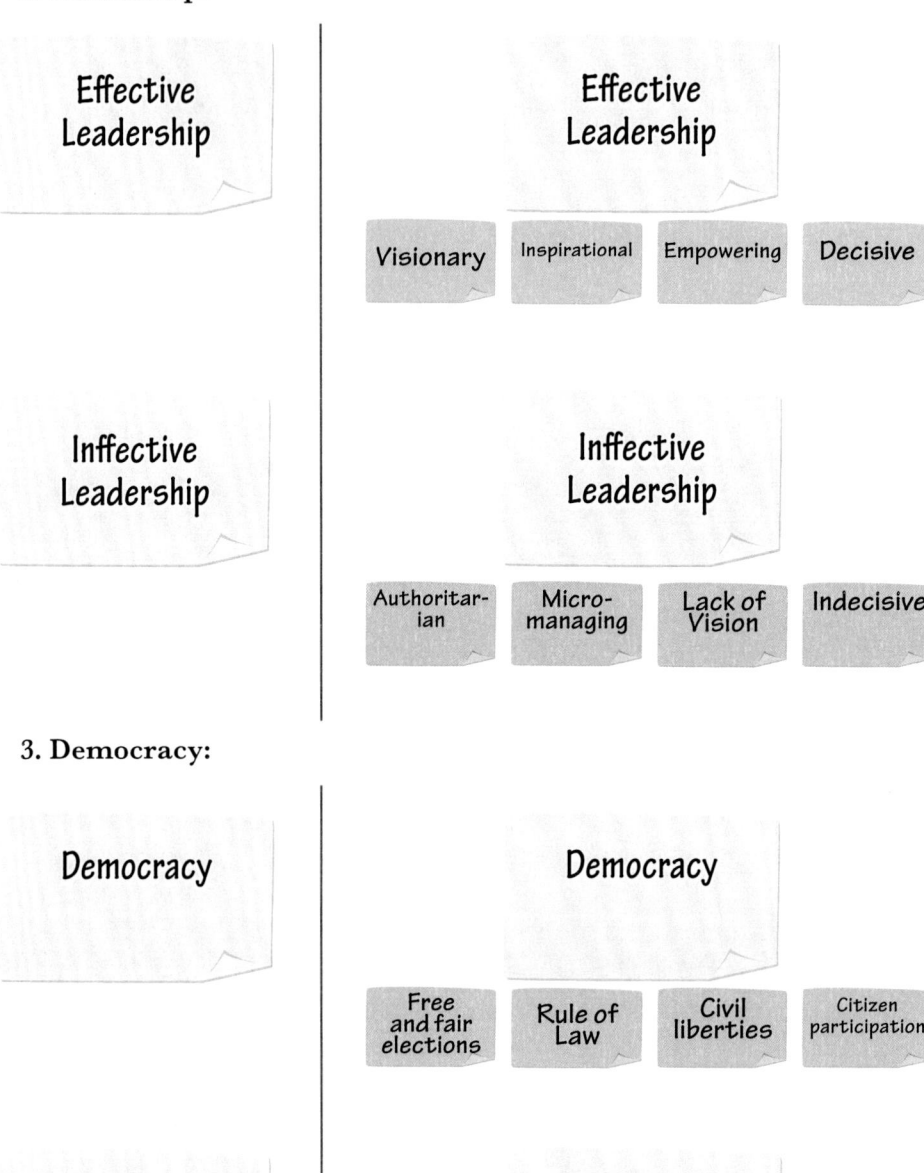

Effective
Leadership

Effective
Leadership

Visionary   Inspirational   Empowering   Decisive

Inffective
Leadership

Inffective
Leadership

Authoritar-ian   Micro-managing   Lack of Vision   Indecisive

3. Democracy:

Democracy

Democracy

Free and fair elections   Rule of Law   Civil liberties   Citizen participation

Non-Democratic
Systems

Non-Democratic
Systems

Authorit-arian regimes   Lack of political freedoms   Supression of dissent   Unelected leaders

4. Sustainability:

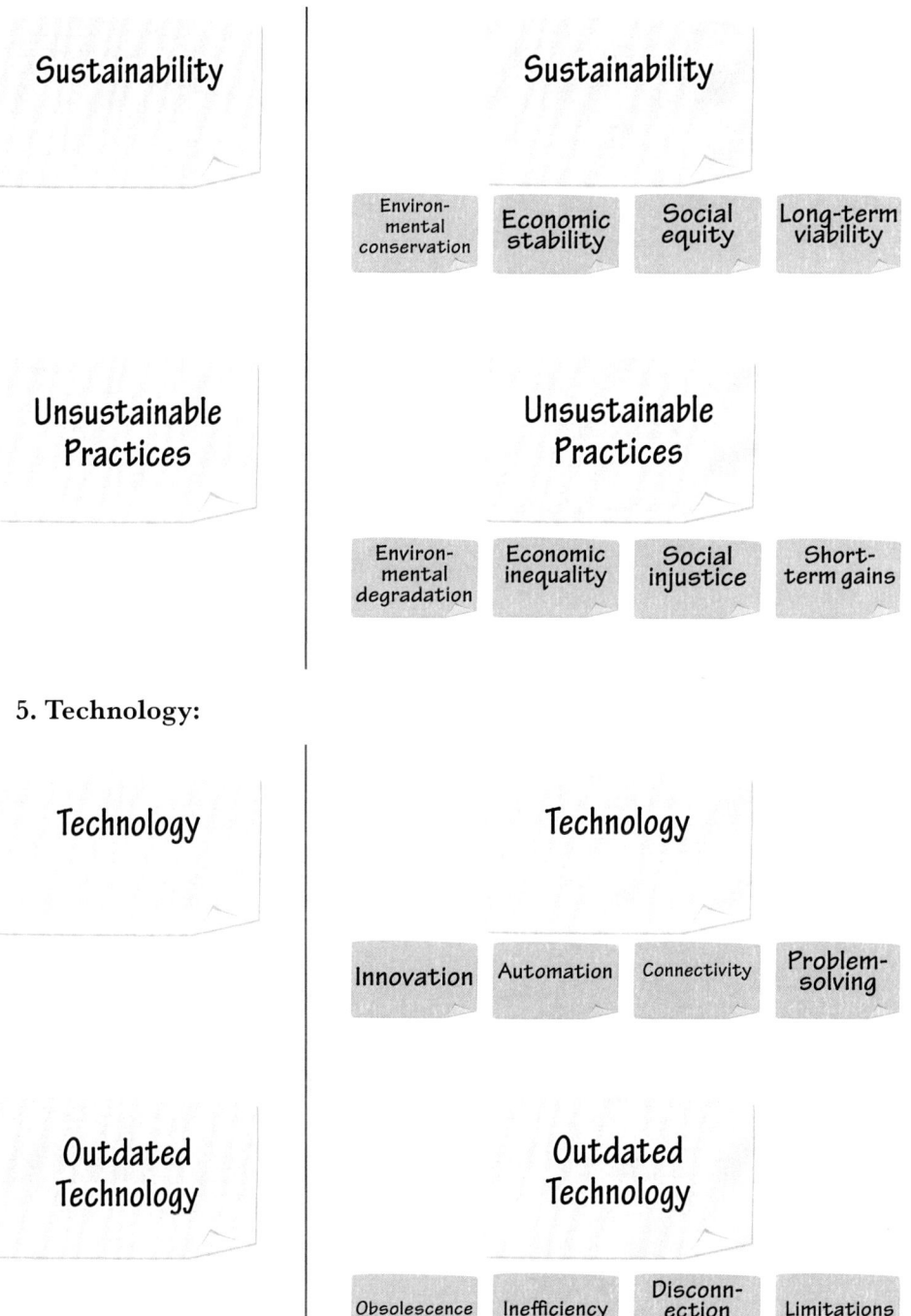

Sustainability

| Sustainability |
| Environ-mental conservation | Economic stability | Social equity | Long-term viability |

Unsustainable Practices

| Unsustainable Practices |
| Environ-mental degradation | Economic inequality | Social injustice | Short-term gains |

5. Technology:

Technology

| Technology |
| Innovation | Automation | Connectivity | Problem-solving |

Outdated Technology

| Outdated Technology |
| Obsolescence | Inefficiency | Disconn-ection | Limitations |

6. Empathy:

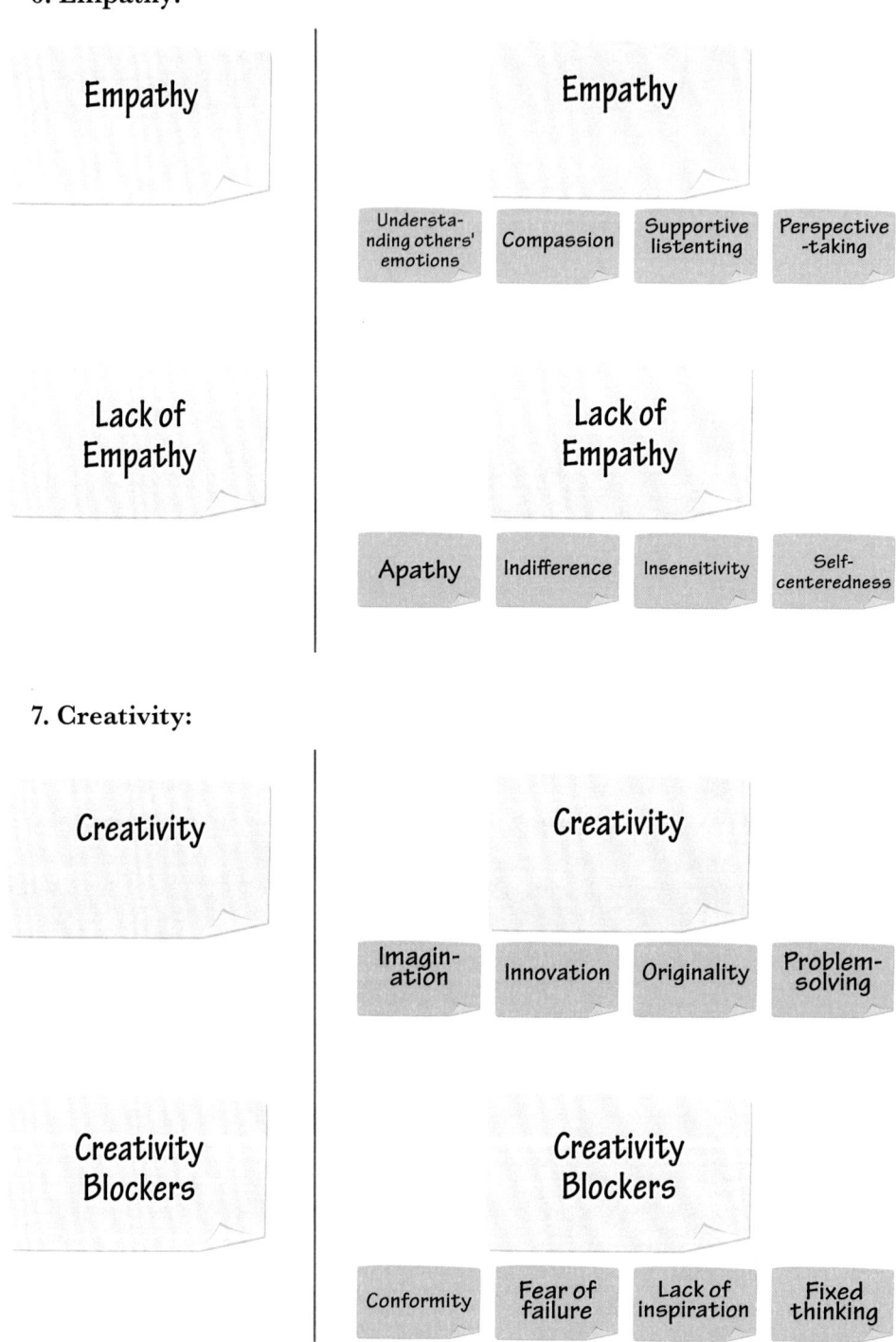

Empathy

Empathy

Understanding others' emotions   Compassion   Supportive listening   Perspective-taking

Lack of Empathy

Lack of Empathy

Apathy   Indifference   Insensitivity   Self-centeredness

7. Creativity:

Creativity

Creativity

Imagination   Innovation   Originality   Problem-solving

Creativity Blockers

Creativity Blockers

Conformity   Fear of failure   Lack of inspiration   Fixed thinking

8. Health:

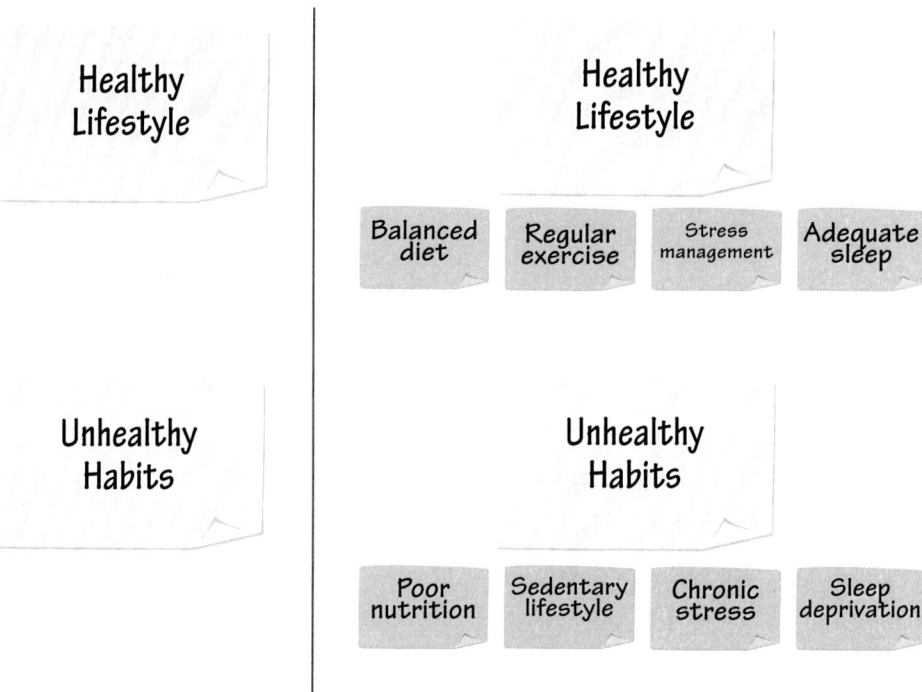

Healthy
Lifestyle

Healthy
Lifestyle

Balanced
diet

Regular
exercise

Stress
management

Adequate
sleep

Unhealthy
Habits

Unhealthy
Habits

Poor
nutrition

Sedentary
lifestyle

Chronic
stress

Sleep
deprivation

9. Conflict Resolution:

Conflict
Resolution

Conflict
Resolution

Effective
communi-
cation

Compromise

Mediation

Problem-
solving

Conflict
Escalation

Conflict
Escalation

Miscomm-
unication

Stubborn-
ness

Escalation

Avoidance

10. Globalization:

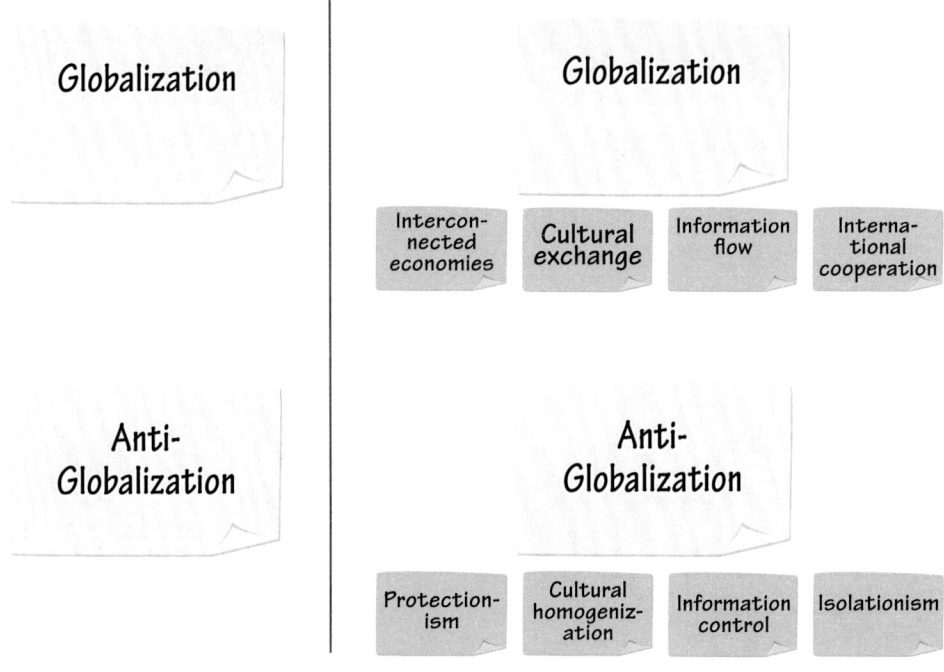

These Is/IsNot Lists provide a structured way to explore and understand each concept by identifying its defining characteristics (identity) and distinguishing it from elements that do not align with the concept (other).

The Ambiguity Trap: A Cautionary Tale Not to Overlook the Is/IsNot List Move in Life and Work

Is/IsNot List Move - Helps users remember to distinguish something by listing both what it is and what it is not attempting to get at what fundamentally makes it different from what it is not. It is fundamentally about the identity-other Distinction (D) pattern of DSRP

Emily, a project manager at a leading software development firm, was known for her efficiency and attention to detail. At work, she was leading a crucial project to develop a new application. In her personal life, she was planning a family reunion, coordinating with various relatives to make the event a success.

In both scenarios, Emily was confident in her communication skills. She believed that her instructions and messages were clear and that everyone was on the same page. However, she overlooked the importance of the Is/IsNot List move, assuming that everyone understood the distinctions she had in mind.

At work, during team meetings, she used terms like "user-friendly" and "intuitive" to describe the desired features of the application. She assumed that her team had a shared understanding of what these terms meant. However, without clear distinctions, each team member had their own interpretation, leading to inconsistent design choices and features that didn't align with Emily's vision.

Similarly, in planning the family reunion, Emily communicated dates, times, and activities using general terms, assuming that her relatives would interpret them as she intended. However, the lack of clear distinctions led to confusion about the schedule, with some relatives arriving on the wrong day and others missing planned activities.

As the project deadline approached and the reunion date neared, the consequences of Emily's oversight became evident. The application development was behind schedule, with significant rework needed to align the features with Emily's original vision. The family reunion, while enjoyable, was marred by logistical issues and misunderstandings.

Realizing her mistake, Emily took a step back and applied the Is/IsNot List move. In her professional life, she convened a team meeting where she clearly defined key terms and concepts, creating a shared understanding of what was expected for the application. She presented a structured format to make the distinctions clear:

User-Friendly

User-Friendly Is		User-Friendly Is Not
* Intuitive navigation	|	* Complex menus
* Simple language	|	* Technical jargon
* Clear instructions	|	* Ambiguous commands
* Minimal steps	|	* Requiring extensive training

In her personal life, for the family reunion, Emily sent out a detailed itinerary using a similar structure:

Welcome Dinner

Welcome Dinner Is		Welcome Dinner Is Not
* Casual dress code	|	* Formal attire required
* Buffet-style meal	|	* Seated dinner
* Starting at 6 PM	|	* Starting earlier in the day

By providing these clear distinctions, Emily ensured that her team had a shared understanding of what was expected for each feature of the application. This helped align their efforts and reduced the need for rework. Similarly, the detailed itinerary for the reunion clarified the expectations for each event, reducing confusion and ensuring that her relatives were prepared for what was planned.

Through these experiences, Emily learned the importance of making clear distinctions and ensuring that everyone involved had a shared understanding of terms and concepts. She recognized that assuming shared meaning without verification could lead to confusion and misalignment, both in her professional and personal life. From that point on, she committed to using the Is/IsNot List move to prevent ambiguity and ensure clarity in all her communications.

Practice

 Use sticky notes, index cards, a dry erase board, or just pen and paper.
Choose a thing—anything—and make a list of what it is and what it is not.
Keep it simple at first: a tree, a team, a goal. Then build toward more abstract
concepts: love, freedom, success. Practice in the car, on a walk, or while
people-watching. The goal is not perfection—it's practice. Burn the neurons
and they'll be there when you need them. With time, your brain will start to do
this move automatically, sharpening your ability to define and discern what truly
matters.

Chapter 9: Zoom In-Zoom Out Move

In a world driven by scientific inquiry and discovery, there existed two distinct categories of scientists: the splitters and the lumpers. Splitters were known for their meticulous analysis, breaking down complex phenomena into smaller, more manageable parts, only to dissect them further. On the other hand, lumpers were the synthesis masters, adept at amalgamating information and seeing the bigger picture.

In this scientific landscape, a new breed of scientists emerged, known as "splumpers." These individuals possessed a unique ability to navigate the delicate balance between splitting and lumping. They recognized that both approaches had their merits and limitations. Splumpers were the amphibians of the scientific world, seamlessly transitioning between the roles of splitters and lumpers as the situation demanded.

Splitters　　　Lumpers

Their value became evident in the face of complex and multifaceted challenges. Whether it was unraveling the intricacies of a biological ecosystem or deciphering the complexities of a global economic crisis, the splumpers thrived. They possessed the versatility to break down intricate systems into their constituent elements when needed, while also having the capacity to synthesize diverse information into a cohesive understanding.

In a world that demanded adaptability and a holistic perspective, the splumpers became the catalysts of innovation and progress. They were the ones who bridged the gap between reductionism and holistic thinking, acknowledging that there was no one-size-fits-all approach to scientific inquiry.

Today, we recognize the invaluable role of splumpers, the scientists who embody the spirit of adaptability and balance. They are the ones who remind us that the most profound discoveries often lie at the intersection of analytical precision and holistic synthesis. In an ever-evolving world, we need more splumpers—those who can split, lump, and seamlessly traverse the boundaries of scientific exploration. Splumpers know how to Zoom In/Zoom Out.

In the journey of understanding complex systems and ideas, one of the most powerful cognitive moves at our disposal is the Zoom In and Zoom Out move. This move empowers us to explore the depths of intricate details while never losing sight of the broader context. It's like having a versatile microscope and a wide-angle lens for our thoughts.

Zooming In: The Microscopic View

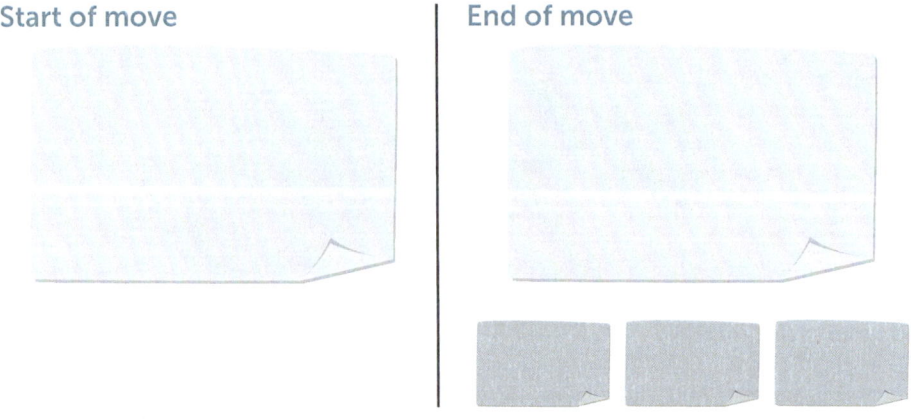

Start of move   End of move

Imagine you're looking at a photograph of a dense forest. When you "Zoom In," you're like a curious scientist examining a single leaf under a microscope. You delve deep into the minutiae, exploring the intricate patterns of veins, the cells' chlorophyll-filled factories, and the ecosystem of microorganisms living on the leaf's surface. This microscopic view reveals the hidden wonders of the leaf, reminding us that even the smallest components play vital roles in the bigger scheme of things.

In real-life scenarios, Zooming In can be applied to various domains. For instance:

- Science: Scientists may Zoom In to study the structure of a single protein molecule, uncovering its role in a complex biological process.

- Literature: Literary analysts Zoom In on a single paragraph or sentence, dissecting its literary devices and nuances to understand the author's intent.

- Business: Business analysts might focus on a single customer interaction to improve the customer experience.

The Zoom In move is a reminder that within the grand tapestry of any system, the devil often resides in the details.

Zooming Out: The Wide-Angle Perspective

Start of move

End of move

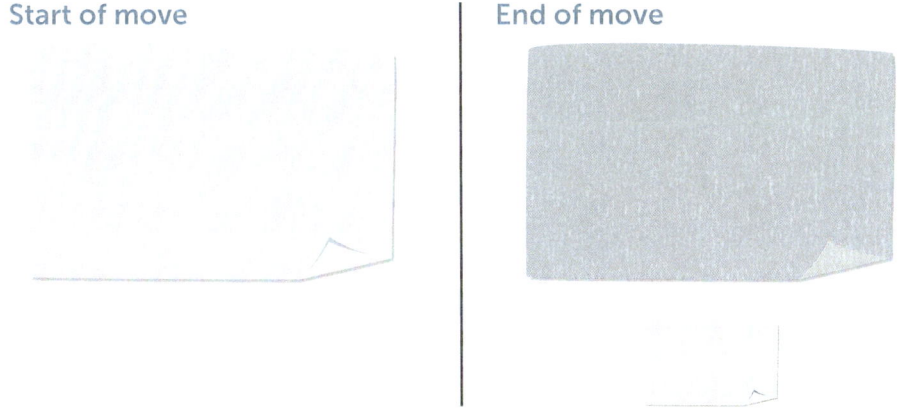

Now, let's consider the forest photograph again. This time, you "Zoom Out" to take in the entire forest, the surrounding landscape, and even the global climate. Zooming Out allows you to see the forest within the context of the world—how it interacts with neighboring ecosystems, influences weather patterns, and connects to broader environmental issues.

In practical terms:

- Ecology: Ecologists Zoom Out to study the role of a specific ecosystem in the global carbon cycle, understanding its impact on climate change.

- History: Historians Zoom Out to analyze a particular event in the context of its era, exploring its socio-political implications on a grand scale.

- Economics: Economists Zoom Out to examine the economic health of a single country within the global market, considering trade, politics, and international relations.

Zooming Out helps us avoid tunnel vision, fostering a holistic understanding of any subject. It reveals patterns, connections, and consequences that might be overlooked in a narrower view.

Balancing Act: Zooming In and Out

The art of systemic thinking often lies in the balance between Zooming In and Zooming Out. It's akin to adjusting the focus of a camera lens to capture the essence of a scene. Knowing when to dive into the details and when to rise above for a broader perspective is a skill that can be applied in various aspects of life. By mastering Zoom In and Zoom Out, we gain the ability to dissect complex problems, appreciate the beauty of intricacies, and grasp the interconnectedness of the world. Whether you're analyzing data, reading a novel, or tackling global challenges, seeing both the smaller and bigger pictures unlocks deeper insights into anything we seek to understand.

Examples

Let's revisit the first example of the Zoom In/Out Move with added parts and wholes, along with text-based maps:

1. Ecosystem Ecology (Professional):

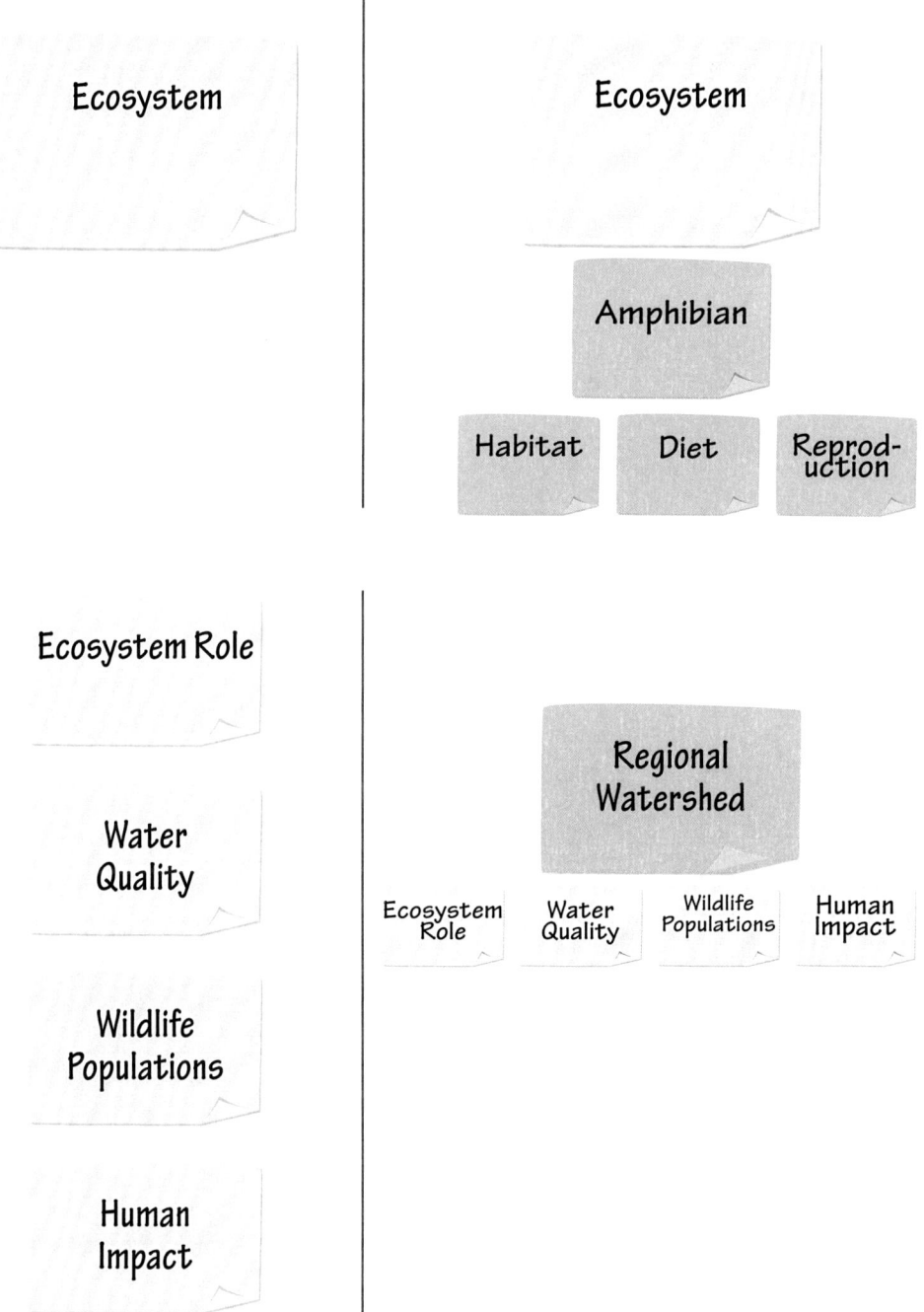

This enhanced example demonstrates how the Zoom In/Out Move can delve into specific parts while maintaining an awareness of the larger whole within the context of ecosystem ecology.

2. Educational Curriculum (Professional):

Math Lesson Plan

Math Lesson Plan

Lesson objectives

Teaching materials

Student engagement

Curriculum Alignment

Educational Standards

Long-term Outcomes

Annual Curriculum

Curriculum Alignment

Educational Standards

Long-term Outcomes

3. Product Design (Professional):

Camera
Module
(Smartphone)

Camera
Module
(Smartphone)

Specific-
ations

Lens
Quality

Image
Processing

Component
Integration

User Experience

Smartphone
Design

Market
Competitiveness

Component
Integration

User Experience

Market
Competit-
iveness

4. Personal Health (Personal):

Daily
Cardio
Workouts

Daily
Cardio
Workouts

Heart Rate

Exercise Type

Duration

Nutrition

Sleep

Stress Management

Long-term Goals

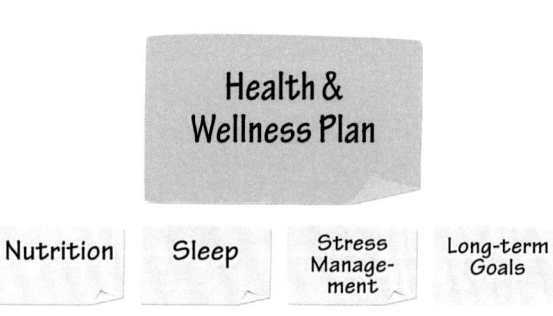

Health & Wellness Plan

Nutrition

Sleep

Stress Management

Long-term Goals

5. Environmental Conservation (Professional and Personal):

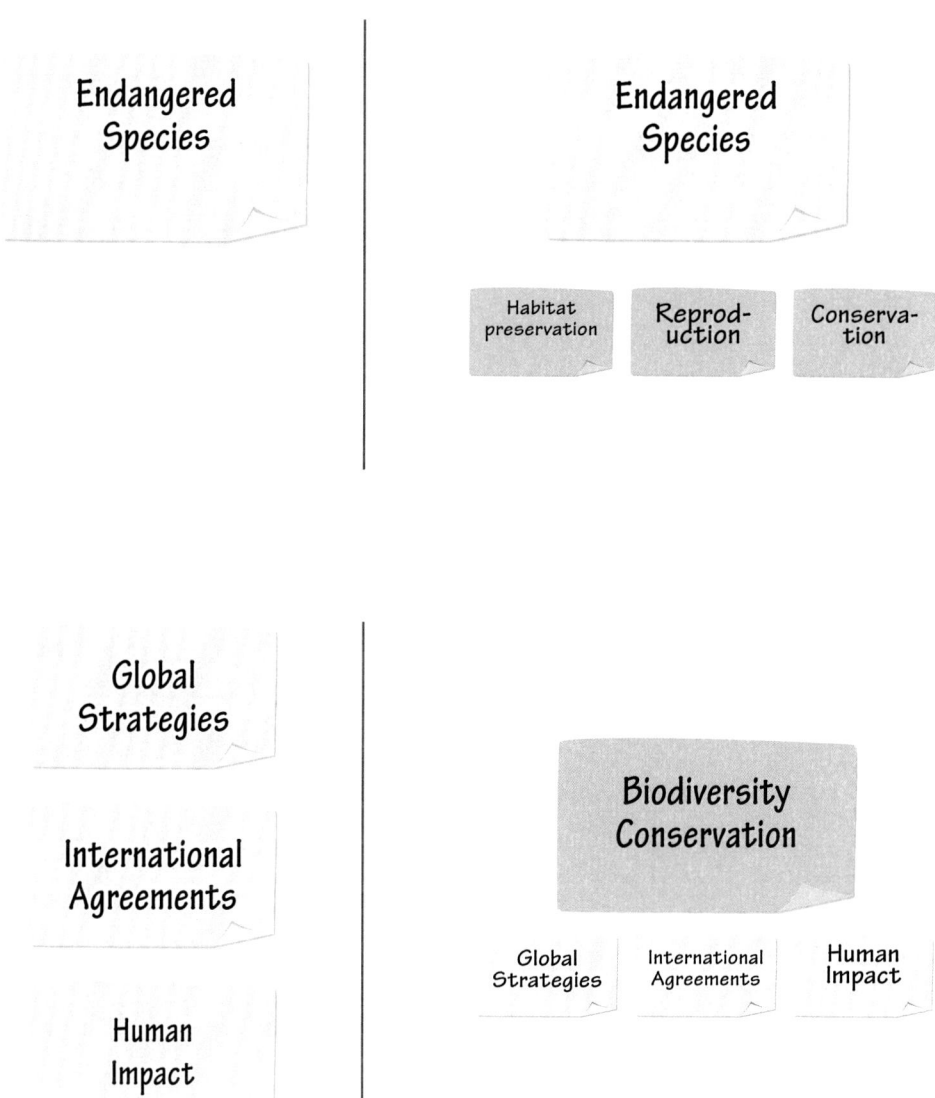

6. Software Development (Professional):

Code
Module

Code
Module

Function-
ality

Algorithms

Testing
Methods

Module
Integration

User
Experience

Project Objectives &
Goals

Software
Architecture

Module
Integration

User
Experience

Project
Objectives &
Goals

These examples illustrate how the Zoom In/Out Move can be applied across various scenarios, providing a deeper understanding of specific parts while considering their role within the larger whole.

The Big Picture Blur: A Cautionary Tale of Forgetting to Zoom In in Life and Work

Zoom In Move – Encourages users to look closely at the parts that make up a thing, allowing for precision, clarity, and understanding how things work.

Martin, while known for his vision and creativity, sometimes missed important details. When he was assigned to redesign a corporate campus, he immediately sketched sweeping concepts that wowed the client—until execution began. At the same time, he started preparing for a family cabin vacation, making broad plans for "fun, nature, and togetherness."

But both plans faltered.

Contractors struggled due to missing specs, dimensions, and misaligned elements. The vacation too became chaotic: the cabin lacked essential supplies, and "fun" activities weren't fully thought out. Martin had failed to Zoom In—to break the project down into its *key parts.*

Realizing this, Martin embraced the Zoom In move. For the building:

Office Building

- Interior Design
- Accessibility
- Energy Efficiency

He specified every detail from fixtures to flow. For the vacation:

Cabin Stay

- Nature Hikes
- Campfires
- Leisurely Meals

He listed the essentials and made sure each activity had what it needed to succeed. From then on, Martin made sure to Zoom In—to understand the parts that made up his ideas. It gave him clarity and control, and made both his work and his home life function better.

Practice

Choose something you experience every day—a conversation, a tool, a feeling—and examine its parts. Then look at the parts of those parts. Keep drilling down until the details become absurdly specific. Use index cards, mind maps, or even just your imagination to break down a cup of coffee into beans, farmers, shipping routes, water temperature, flavor notes, mug choice. Train your mind to go deeper, finer, more granular. You'll soon notice your attention sharpening. Zooming in is about finding the invisible complexity hidden inside the obvious. Remember: The goal is not perfection—it's practice. Burn the neurons and they'll be there when you need them.

The Detail Trap: A Cautionary Tale of Forgetting to Zoom Out in Life and Work

Zoom Out Move – Helps users step back to see the larger system a thing is a part of, allowing for context, purpose, and big-picture clarity.

Martin, a seasoned architect, was renowned for his precision and detail. When asked to design a new office building for a major client, he immersed himself in the details—materials, finishes, ergonomic layouts, and sustainability features. Simultaneously, Martin meticulously planned a family vacation, filling each day with hikes, kayaking, and local excursions.

But in both cases, Martin failed to Zoom Out.

The building, though beautifully designed, clashed with the surrounding cityscape and created unexpected traffic congestion. His family, excited for a break, instead felt stressed by the relentless itinerary. He had failed to step back and consider the larger system—the neighborhood, the city, the client's values, and most importantly, the broader *purpose* of the vacation: relaxation and reconnection.

Realizing his mistake, Martin decided to Zoom Out. For the building, he reevaluated it as part of a greater system:

Cityscape

    Community

       Office Building

He adjusted the design to complement the community, include green space, and align with the city's vision. For his vacation, he reframed it under the purpose of family well-being:

Quality Time

    Relaxation

       Cabin Stay

He trimmed the schedule, allowed room for spontaneity, and prioritized ease over efficiency.

From that point on, Martin adopted the Zoom Out move whenever he planned anything. He discovered that by seeing the forest instead of just the trees, his designs—and his relationships—flourished.

Practice

Take any item, event, or idea and ask yourself: what bigger thing is this a part of? And what is that a part of? Use sticky notes, a whiteboard, or just a walk around the block to explore upward connections. For example, your morning routine → your day → your week → your year → your values. Or your dog → your home → your neighborhood → your city ecosystem. Push past the usual scope. Train your mind to widen its lens. Zooming out builds the ability to see broader impacts, context, and systems that shape what's in front of you. Remember: The goal is not perfection—it's practice. Burn the neurons and they'll be there when you need them.

Chapter 10: Part-Party! Move

Just like you and I enjoy a good party, parts have their own way of celebrating. They, too, like to come together and interact, just as we do when we dance, talk, and have a great time at gatherings. So, imagine the world of parts as a grand celebration, where each piece plays its role and joins in the festivities. Just as you help create a lively atmosphere at a party, you can help parts relate and dance in harmony. So, let's join the parts in their celebration and make the party even more vibrant!

In the journey of developing structural metacognition, we encounter a fascinating cognitive move known as the Part Party! Move. This move invites us to delve into the intricate relationships that exist within a whole, breaking it down into its constituent parts and investigating how these parts relate to one another. By engaging in this move, we gain deeper insights into the underlying structures and connections that shape our understanding of various phenomena, from complex systems to everyday objects.

The Part Party! Move is rooted in the fundamental concept of systems thinking, where everything is viewed as a system composed of interconnected parts. It encourages us to recognize that within any whole, there exists a multitude of parts, each playing a distinct role in shaping the whole's functionality.

The Process of Part Party!

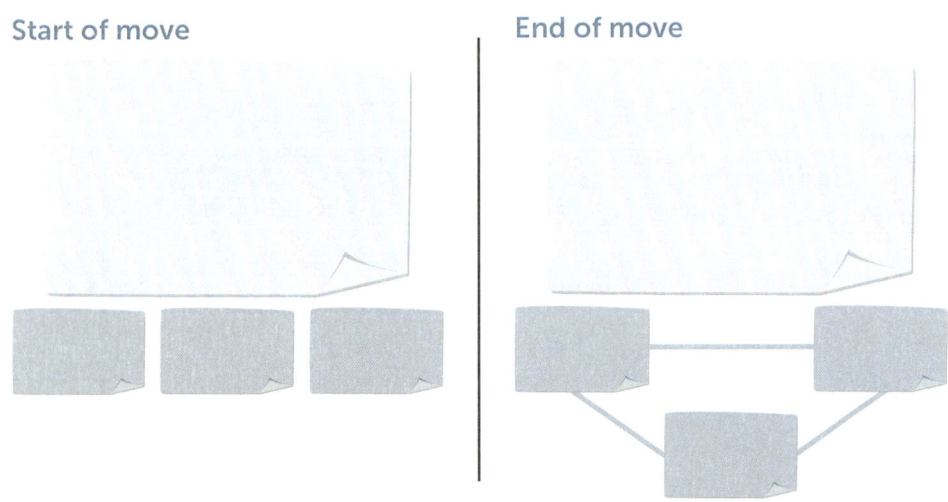

Start of move | End of move

When undertaking the Part Party! Move, the process is straightforward but enlightening:

- Identify the Whole: Begin by selecting a whole, which can be anything from a biological organism to a societal structure or even an abstract concept.

- List the Parts: Next, dissect the whole into its constituent parts, naming each part along the way. This step requires careful observation and consideration.

- Discover Relationships: Now comes the intriguing part—examine how these parts interact and relate to one another within the whole.

Are there dependencies, hierarchies, or feedback loops? Identify the connections that make the whole function as it does.

- Reflect on Significance: Finally, reflect on the significance of these relationships. How do they contribute to the overall behavior or understanding of the whole? What insights can you derive from this exploration?

The Part Party! Move finds its utility across a wide range of domains and disciplines. In biology, it aids in understanding the intricate web of interactions within ecosystems. In engineering, it facilitates the analysis of complex systems by breaking them down into manageable components. In psychology, it can reveal the interplay between different cognitive processes.

Engaging in the Part Party! Move not only enhances our analytical thinking but also promotes a deeper appreciation for the interconnectedness of the world around us. It enables us to see the big picture while appreciating the finer details. This move fosters a holistic perspective, allowing us to make more informed decisions, solve complex problems, and gain a richer understanding of the systems that shape our lives.

The Part Party! Move invites us to embark on a journey of exploration within the world of systems and structures. By dissecting wholes into their constituent parts and deciphering the relationships that bind them, we gain a profound understanding of the underlying complexities that define our reality. This move is a powerful tool for enhancing our cognitive abilities and fostering a more profound appreciation for the intricate tapestry of existence.

Part Party! Examples

These text-based maps illustrate the relationships within each example, showcasing how the Part Party! Move helps dissect wholes into their constituent parts and explore the intricate connections between them.

1. Ecological Systems:

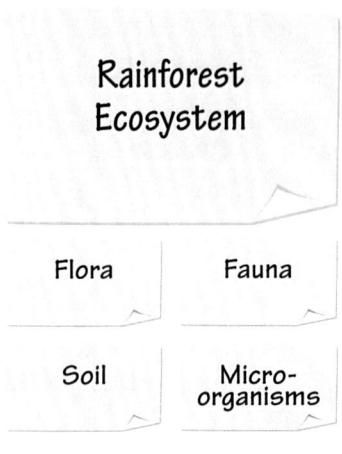

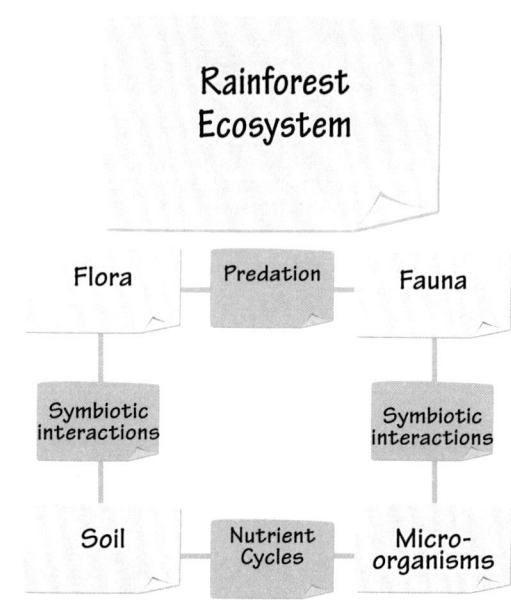

2. Mechanical Watch:

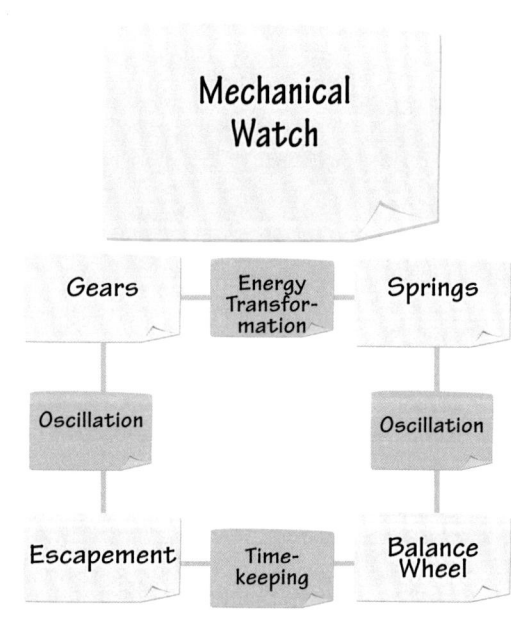

3. History of Civilazation:

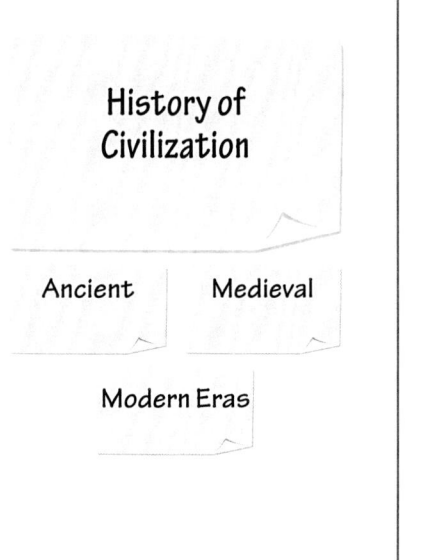
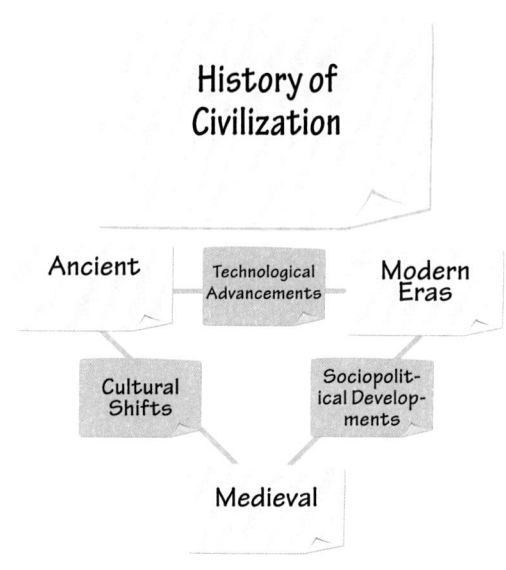

4. Personal Growth:

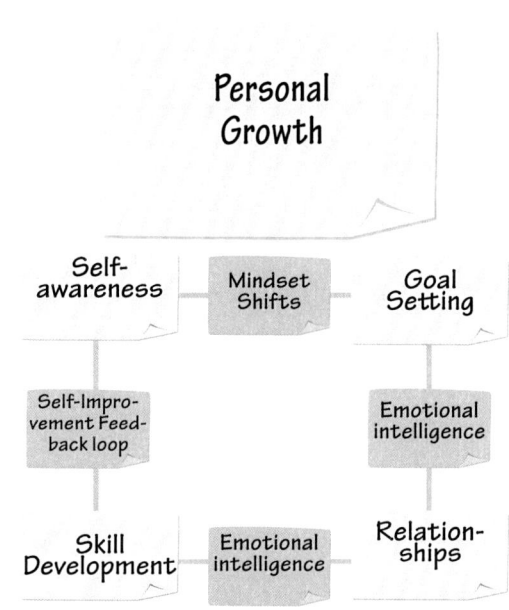

5. Financial Portfolio:

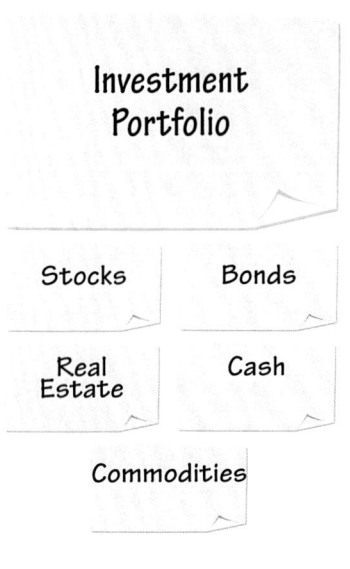

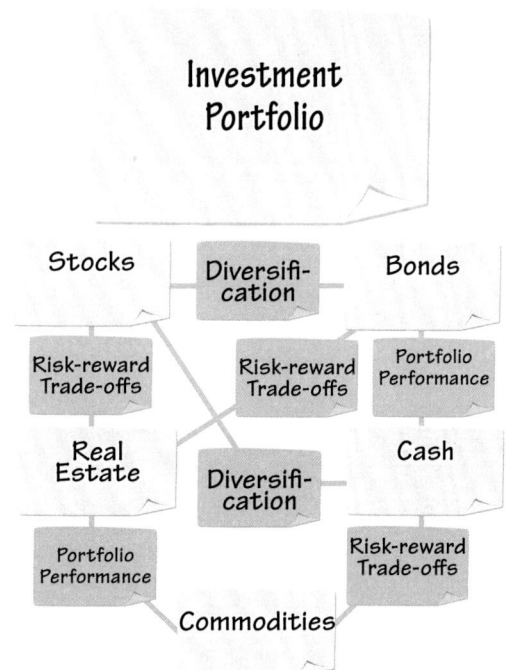

6. Urban Transportation:

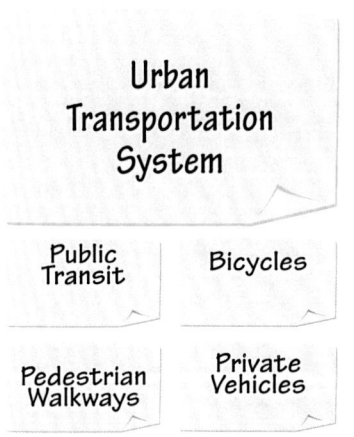

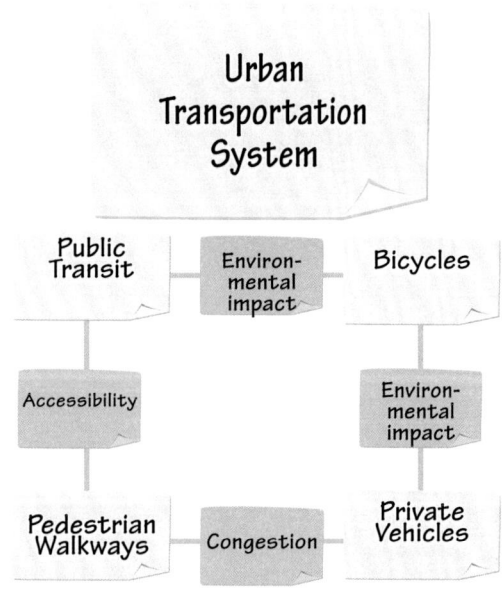

7. Literature Analysis:

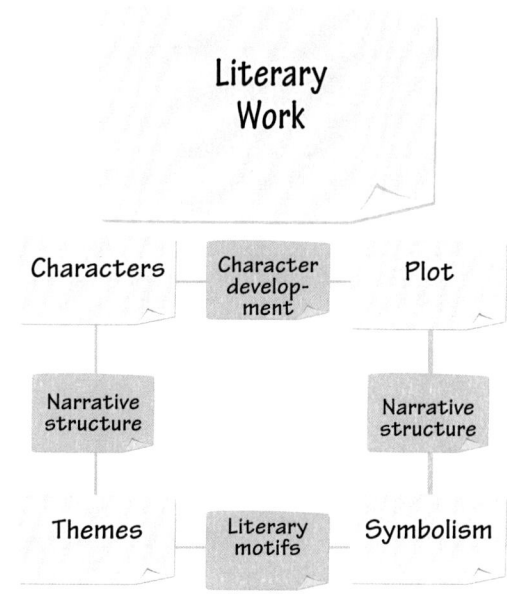

8. Healthcare System:

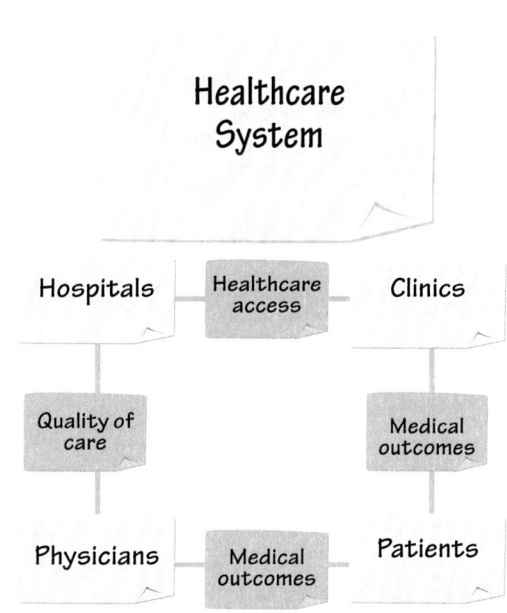

9. Food Nutrition:

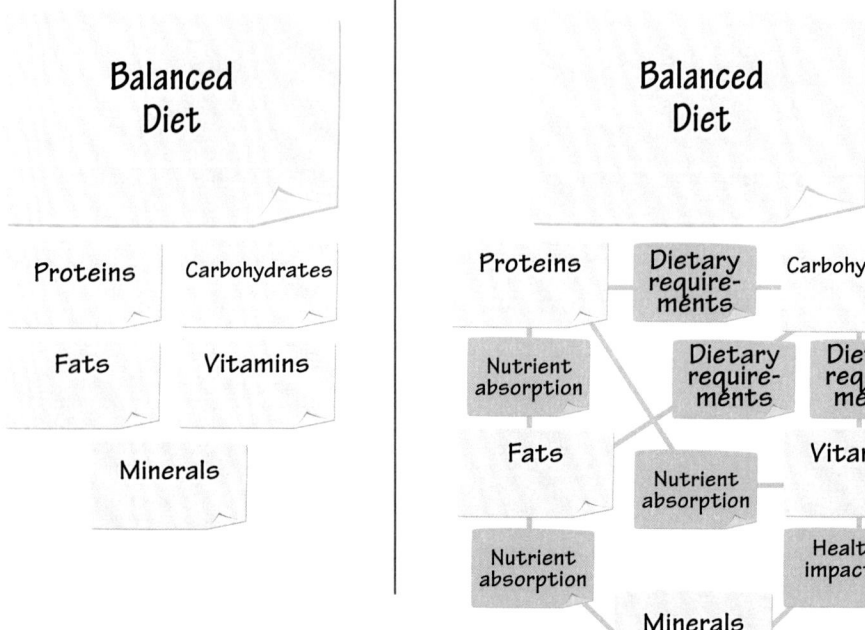

Balanced Diet

Proteins · Carbohydrates
Fats · Vitamins
Minerals

Balanced Diet

Proteins · Dietary requirements · Carbohydrates
Nutrient absorption · Dietary requirements · Dietary requirements
Fats · Vitamins
Nutrient absorption
Nutrient absorption · Health impacts
Minerals

10. Space Exploration:

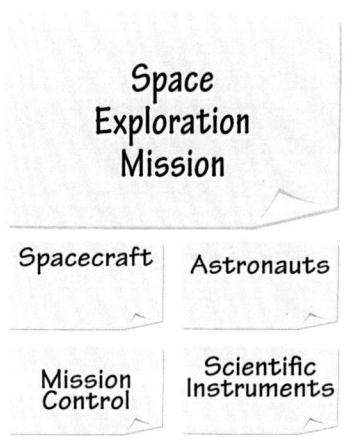

Space Exploration Mission

Spacecraft · Astronauts
Mission Control · Scientific Instruments

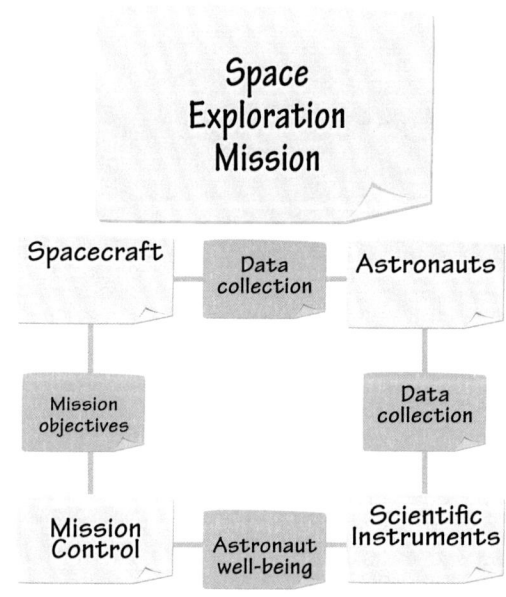

Space Exploration Mission

Spacecraft · Data collection · Astronauts
Mission objectives · Data collection
Mission Control · Astronaut well-being · Scientific Instruments

The Missed Connection: A Cautionary Tale Not to Overlook the Part-Party! Move in Life and Work

Part-Party! - Helps users to remember that once they've Zoomed in on the parts of something they must remember to relate the parts. It's about seeing the relationships exist between the parts. Its especially important in establishing that most effects are the result of a web of causes (not a singular or root cause) so looking at how things are related are important. It is fundamentally about manipulating the action-reaction Relationships (R) pattern of DSRP.

John, a seasoned project manager at a bustling tech firm, prided himself on his ability to see the big picture. With years of experience under his belt, he felt confident that he could handle any project thrown his way. So, when his company landed a major contract to develop a cutting-edge software solution for a high-profile client, John was the natural choice to lead the project.

Parallelly, in his personal life, John was planning a major renovation of his family home. He envisioned a beautiful, modern space that would meet all their needs. In both his professional and personal projects, John focused on the end goals, laying out plans and setting deadlines without delving into the finer details.

However, as both projects kicked off, John overlooked a crucial step: breaking them down into smaller, manageable parts and understanding how they interacted with each other. He didn't bother with the Part-Party! move, dismissing it as unnecessary detail work that would only slow things down.

As the software project progressed, problems began to surface. The team encountered unexpected technical challenges, communication breakdowns, and integration issues. Without a clear understanding of how the different parts of the software were supposed to interact, they struggled to find effective solutions. Similarly, in his home renovation, contractors faced issues with incompatible materials and design elements that didn't fit together as expected, leading to delays and escalating costs.

In a last-ditch effort to salvage both situations, John reluctantly decided to apply the Part-Party! move. He and his team took a step back and meticulously broke down the software into its component parts, creating a word map to visualize the relationships:

Software Project

Relationships:

User Interface --------> Functionality

Functionality --------> Integration

Functionality --------> Performance

Integration   --------> Security

Simultaneously, for his home renovation, John created a similar map to understand the relationships between different aspects of the project:

Home Renovation

Relationships:

Design   --------> Functionality

Functionality --------> Aesthetics

Functionality --------> Efficiency

Efficiency   --------> Comfort

These maps helped John see how the User Interface and Functionality in the software project were interlinked, and how Design and Functionality in his home renovation were crucial for achieving Aesthetics and Comfort. By understanding these relationships, he could identify the root causes of the problems in both areas and develop targeted solutions.

The software project and home renovation slowly got back on track, but the damage was done. The delays and cost overruns had tarnished John's professional reputation and strained his family's patience. John realized, too late, that his initial failure to use the Part-Party! move had been a costly mistake in both his work and personal life. From that point on, he vowed never to underestimate the importance of breaking down and understanding the parts of any project, no matter how confident he felt in his big-picture vision.

Practice

This is your invitation to the mental party of systems. Take anything around you—your phone, your breakfast, your team—and list all its parts. Now ask: how are those parts connected? Do they interact? Could some be missing? Are they ordered or chaotic? Practice with simple systems (a bike), living systems (a friendship), or complex ones (immigration). Use sticky notes, draw it out, or build it with objects. The more you explore part-whole relationships and how the parts party together, the more you'll start seeing systems everywhere—and spotting what's missing in them. Remember: The goal is not perfection—it's practice. Burn the neurons and they'll be there when you need them.

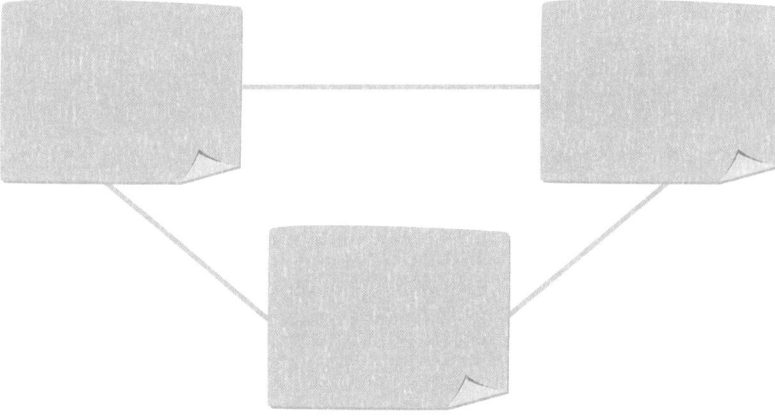

Chapter 11: RDS Barbell Move

Imagine the day you called in a plumber to work his magic on your new sink installation. You knew the task at hand was to connect your sleek sink basin to the wall, and you were counting on a professional to get the job done right.

As the plumber arrived, you explained the situation, emphasizing the importance of securely connecting the sink to the wall. With a nod, he set to work. You watched with anticipation, expecting a meticulous and precise approach to the task.

To your bewilderment, the plumber did something entirely unexpected. He pulled out a massive, black sharpie marker from his toolbox and casually drew a thick, black line from the sink to the wall. Proudly, he turned to you and announced, "That'll be $200 dollars."

You couldn't believe your eyes. The simplicity and inadequacy of this "solution" left you utterly baffled. You wouldn't tolerate such shoddy work from a plumber, and rightly so. Just as you wouldn't accept this quick fix, we shouldn't settle for shoddy thinking either.

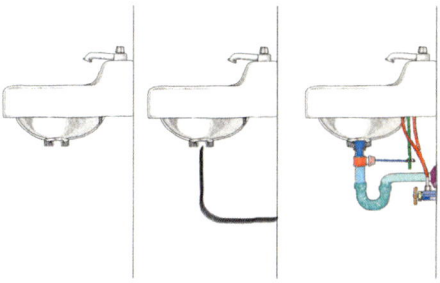

This whimsical encounter highlights a crucial lesson in understanding relationships. The plumber's misguided attempt mirrors a common pitfall in our thinking processes—superficially acknowledging relationships without delving into their intricate components.

To truly comprehend and appreciate relationships, we must take a page from the plumber's manual. Just as he needed to understand and assemble the actual parts of the plumbing connection—pipe segments, couplings, elbows, and straightaways—we too must recognize and build the genuine components of relationships.

Enter the Relationship Distinction System (RDS), the tool that ensures relationships receive the meticulous attention they deserve. Just as the plumber needed to envision and connect every physical part of the plumbing system, we must recognize that every relationship in nature is an RDS.

Whether it's the plumbing system connecting your sink to the wall or the intricate web of connections in the natural world, RDS reminds us that relationships are not mere black lines drawn with a marker. They are composed of myriad parts, each playing a vital role in the functional interplay between entities.

So, the next time you encounter a problem that involves relationships, remember the plumber's lesson. Embrace the depth and complexity of relationships, just as he had to account for every pipe segment and coupling. By understanding and appreciating the genuine parts of the relationship, you'll be equipped to tackle even the most intricate challenges that come your way.

In our journey to uncover the nuances of metacognition and structural thinking, we encounter a powerful cognitive tool known as the Relationship Distinction System (RDS) move. This move, within the DSRP framework, enables us to dissect and understand the intricate relationships between elements, shedding light on the dynamic interplay of identities, others, and the multifaceted world around us.

Unpacking Relationships:

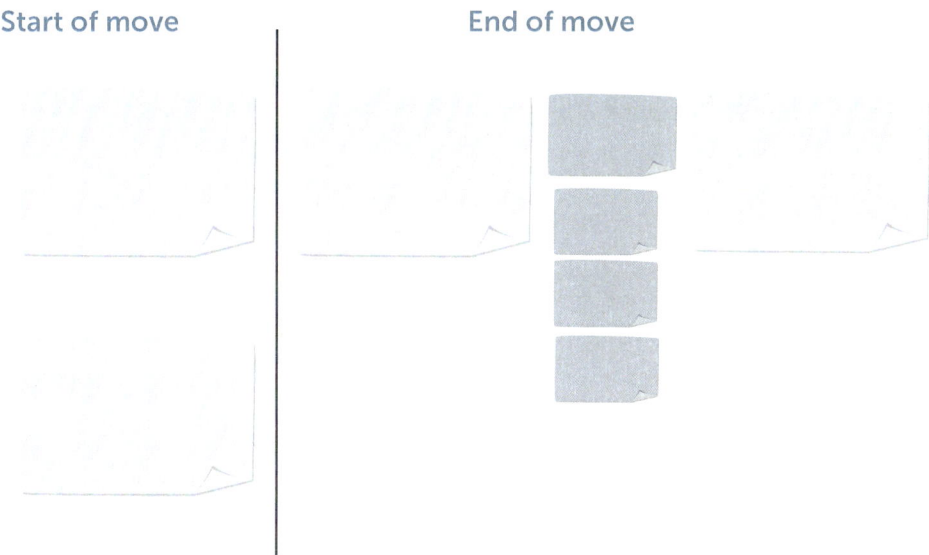

At its core, the RDS move encourages us to delve into the intricacies of relationships, which are omnipresent in our lives. Every interaction, connection, or association between elements can be examined through the lens of RDS. Whether it's the symbiotic relationship between species in an ecosystem, the dynamics between colleagues in a workplace, or the connections in a complex supply chain, the RDS move unveils the underlying structures.

Four Key Elements:

To grasp the essence of RDS, we must acquaint ourselves with its four fundamental elements:

> Identity (i): The identity represents an element or entity at the heart of the relationship. It is the focal point around which the interaction revolves.

> Other (o): The other stands as the counterpart to the identity. It is the element or entity external to the identity, participating in the relationship.

> Action (a): Action signifies the activities, processes, or events

initiated by the identity within the relationship. It showcases what the identity does.

Reaction (r): Reaction portrays the responses, consequences, or effects provoked by the actions of the identity. It highlights how the other reacts to the identity's actions.

The RDS Move in Action:

Imagine you're exploring the intricate world of a coffee supply chain. The coffee farmer, representing the identity, engages in various actions like cultivating, harvesting, and processing coffee beans. These actions have repercussions on the coffee supply chain, which includes other elements such as fair trade practices, transportation logistics, and consumer preferences.

Through the RDS move, you can visualize this complex relationship:

Identity --- **Relationship** --- **Other**
Coffee Farmer --- Coffee Supply Chain --- Coffee Consumer

As you dissect this system, you begin to recognize the interplay between the identity (the coffee farmer), the other (the coffee consumer), the actions (cultivating, harvesting, processing), and the reactions (preferences, demand) within this intricate web.

Applications and Insights:

The RDS move serves as a cognitive tool to make sense of intricate systems, dissect complex relationships, and gain deeper insights into the world around us. By identifying the key elements and their interactions, we can analyze, understand, and even optimize these relationships. Whether in environmental science, organizational dynamics, or social interactions, the RDS move empowers us to navigate the complexities of our interconnected world.

In summary, the Relationship Distinction System (RDS) move equips us with a lens to scrutinize relationships, uncover hidden structures, and foster a deeper understanding of the elements that shape our reality. It invites us to embark on a journey of discovery, where every interaction becomes an opportunity to unveil the underlying dynamics of our interconnected world.

RDS Move Examples

1. Coffee Supply Chain (Farmer to Consumer):

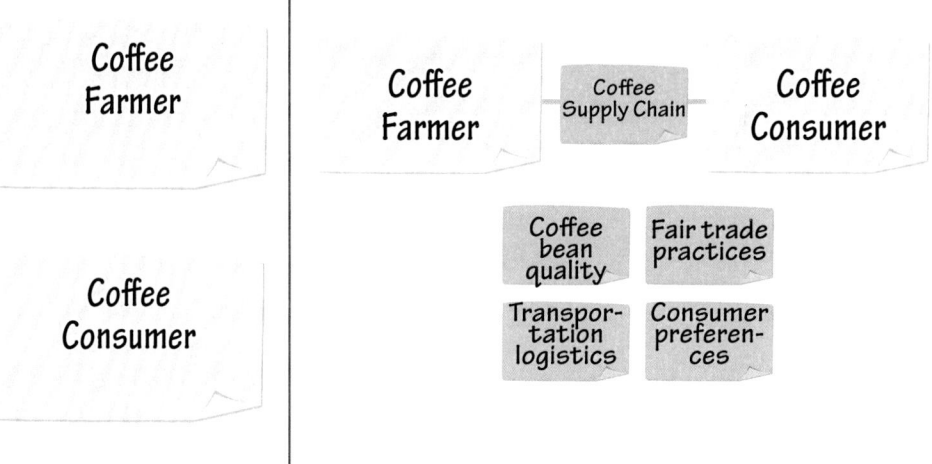

2. Bike Chain (Sprokets):

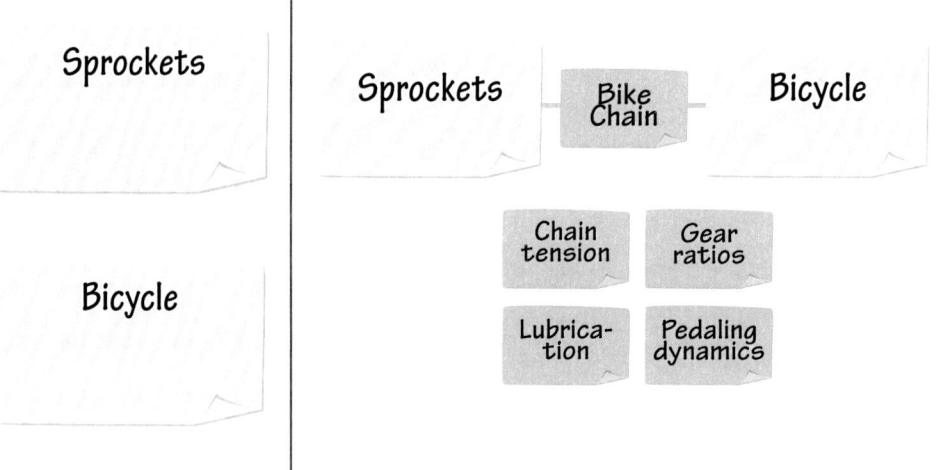

3. Silos in Large Organizations:

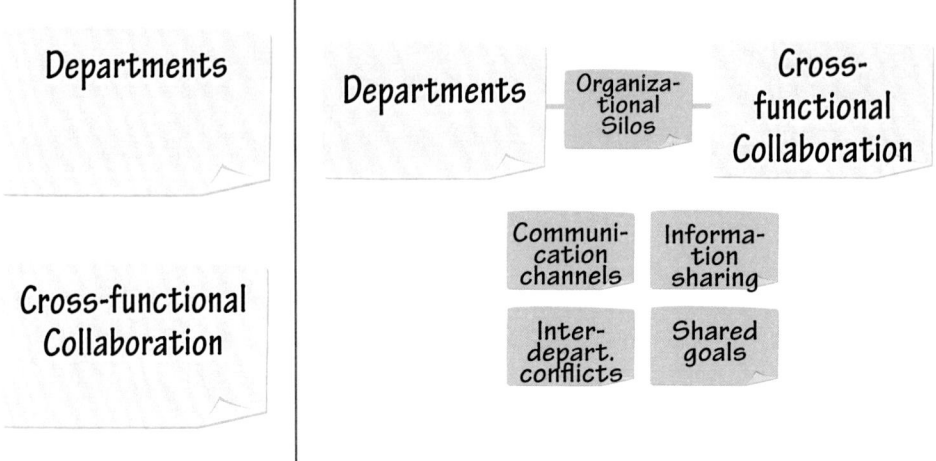

4. Water Cycle (Precipitation to Evaporation):

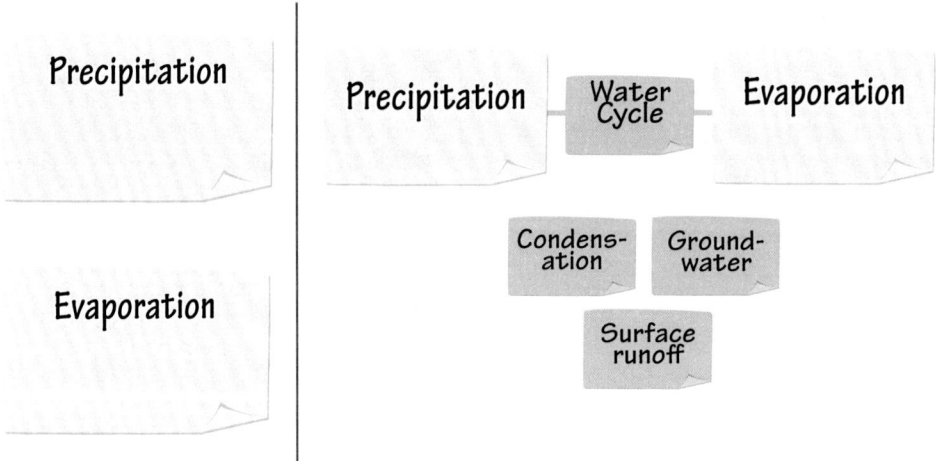

5. Supply and Demand (Producers to Consumers):

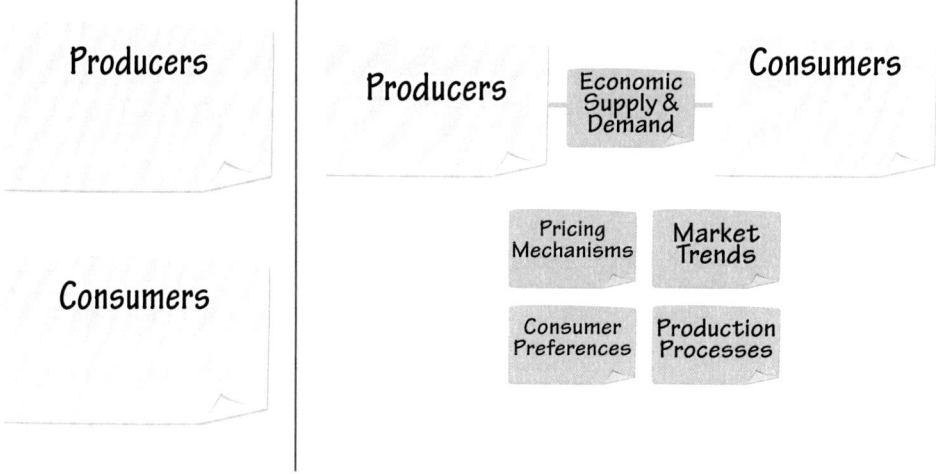

The Unseen Connection: A Cautionary Tale Not to Neglect the RDS Barbell Move in Life and Work

RDS Barbell Move - Stands for "Relationship, Distinction, Systems Barbell." The barbell reference is that it helps users whenever they are looking at the relationship between two things (like a barbell). This Relationship (R) is not merely a relationship but is also a distinct thing so it needs to be named and distinguished. We can also zoom into it and see the part of the relationship. It is fundamentally about manipulating the action-reaction Relationships (R), identity-other Distinction (D), and part-whole Systems (S) pattern of DSRP. In many ways it is borrowing the simplified version of Is/IsNot List Move by naming the relationship and Zoom In Move by listing its parts.

David, a seasoned marketing executive, prided himself on his strategic thinking and ability to forge strong partnerships. At work, he was in the midst of negotiating a crucial deal with a new client, which promised to be a game-changer for his company. At home, he was navigating the complexities of his teenage son's rebellious phase, trying to find common ground.

In both situations, David focused solely on the end goals: securing the client deal and ensuring his son stayed on the right path. He didn't bother to zoom into the relationships at play or use the RDS Barbell move to distinguish and understand the dynamics involved.

In his professional world, David pushed for a contract that favored his company, neglecting to consider the client's perspective and needs. He assumed that the strength of his proposal would be enough to seal the deal. However, he failed to recognize the growing tension and dissatisfaction from the client's side, dismissing their concerns as minor hurdles.

Simultaneously, at home, David imposed strict rules on his son, believing that discipline was the key to resolving his rebellious behavior. He didn't take the time to understand the underlying issues driving his son's actions or to consider his son's point of view.

As the weeks passed, the consequences of David's neglect became apparent. The client, feeling undervalued and misunderstood, decided to back out of the deal at the last minute, leaving David's company scrambling. Meanwhile, his son, feeling unheard and restricted, rebelled even more, straining their relationship further.

It was only then that David realized his mistake. He had failed to zoom into the relationships and distinguish their nuances using the RDS Barbell move. Determined to rectify his errors, David began to apply the RDS Barbell move in both areas.

In his professional life, he revisited the client negotiation with a new approach. He created an RDS map to better understand the dynamics:

David   <---Client Partnership--->   Client
            * Communication
            * Expectations
            * Trust

This map helped David see that Communication, Expectations, and Trust were key components of the Client Partnership. By focusing on these parts, he could rebuild the relationship with the client and address their concerns.

In his personal life, he applied a similar approach to his relationship with his son:

David <---Parent-Child Bond---> Son

         * Listening
         * Understanding
         * Respect

This map showed David that Listening, Understanding, and Respect were crucial for strengthening the Parent-Child Bond. He realized that by prioritizing these aspects, he could reconnect with his son and address the underlying issues in their relationship.

Through these efforts, David managed to salvage the client relationship and gradually rebuild trust with his son. He learned a valuable lesson: neglecting to zoom into and understand the relationships in his life, both professional and personal, could have far-reaching negative consequences. From that point on, he committed to using the RDS Barbell move to ensure he never overlooked the importance of relationship dynamics again.

Practice

This move makes big brain biceps. Pick any two things that seem connected—cause and effect, question and answer, actor and outcome. Map them as a barbell: what's happening on each end, and what connects them in the middle? Are the relationships simple or complex? One-way or two-way? Direct or hidden? Then Zoom into the relationship and see its parts. Give the relationship a name (distinguish it). Practice this move during arguments, when watching the news, or in your own habits. Once you build this muscle, you'll start noticing invisible forces at play—how things influence each other in lines and loops. Remember: The goal is not perfection—it's practice. Burn the neurons and they'll be there when you need them.

Chapter 12: P-Circle Move

Perspective-Circle Move

In our journey through the world of DSRP moves, we've encountered distinct ways of thinking that help us navigate and understand complex relationships. Distinctions, Systems, Relationships, and Part-Whole thinking have all played crucial roles in expanding our cognitive toolbox. Now, as we delve into the fascinating realm of the P-Circle, we're about to discover a move that adds a unique layer to our understanding of perspectives.

The P-Circle, short for Perspective Circle, is all about recognizing the diverse viewpoints and angles from which we can observe and interpret the world around us. It encourages us to embrace the richness of multiple perspectives, each offering its own insights and truths.

Imagine standing in the center of a circle, where you are the focal point. Around you, like points on a compass, are different perspectives—North, South, East, and West. Each direction represents a unique viewpoint, a distinct way of looking at things.

Start of move   **End of move**

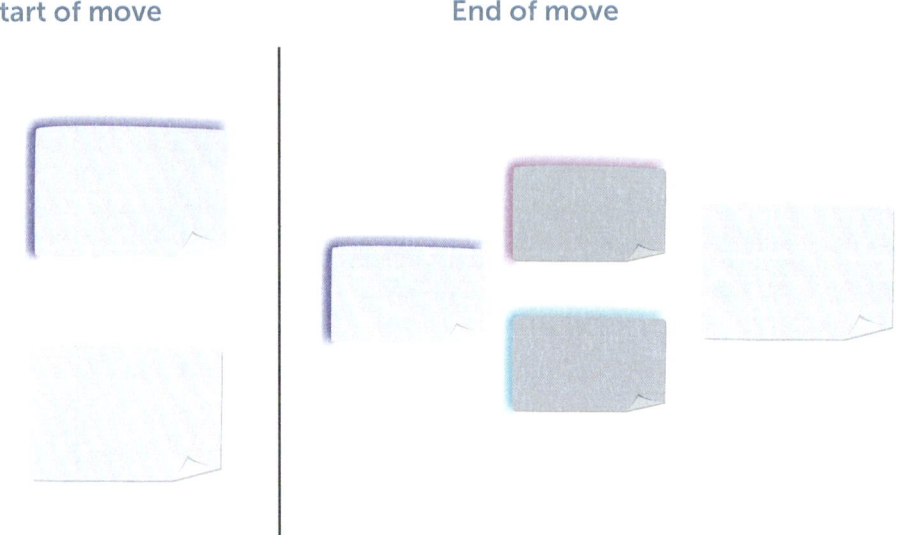

Let's take an example to illustrate the power of the P-Circle. Consider a heated debate about a controversial topic, such as climate change. In the traditional approach, people often fall into opposing camps, each defending their own perspective vehemently. But the P-Circle urges us to step outside our comfort zones and explore the viewpoints of others.

As we move around the P-Circle, we encounter various perspectives. To the North, there's the scientific perspective, grounded in data and evidence. To the South, we find the economic perspective, concerned with the impact on industries and markets. East brings us the ecological perspective, focusing on the planet's health, while West offers the social perspective, highlighting how communities are affected.

By moving around the P-Circle and considering these diverse viewpoints, we gain a more holistic understanding of the issue. We start to see the interconnectedness of these perspectives and how they influence one another. Instead of debating in isolation, we engage in a constructive dialogue that seeks common ground and solutions that benefit everyone.

The P-Circle reminds us that no single perspective holds all the answers.

It encourages us to be open-minded and empathetic, to listen and learn from others, and to appreciate the complexity of the world we live in. By embracing the P-Circle, we become more thoughtful, well-rounded thinkers who can navigate the intricacies of our interconnected reality.

As we continue our journey, remember the P-Circle and the valuable lessons it imparts. It's a reminder that every viewpoint adds a piece to the puzzle, and by weaving these pieces together, we gain a clearer, more comprehensive picture of the world. So, let's step into the P-Circle and explore the myriad perspectives waiting to be discovered.

P-Circle Examples
1. Environmental Conservation:

In the realm of environmental conservation, the P-Circle involves understanding the perspectives of scientists, policymakers, indigenous communities, and corporations. Each viewpoint contributes to the complex web of decisions and actions needed to protect our planet.

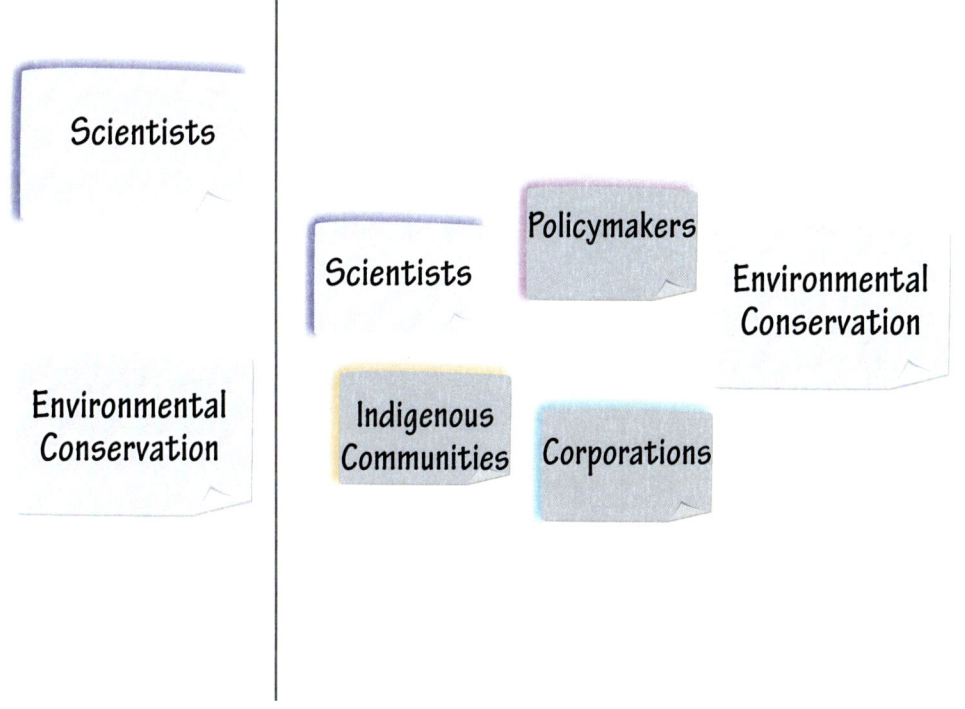

2. Healthcare Policy:

When crafting healthcare policies, it's crucial to consider the perspectives of patients, healthcare providers, insurance companies, and government agencies. These diverse viewpoints help create comprehensive and equitable healthcare solutions.

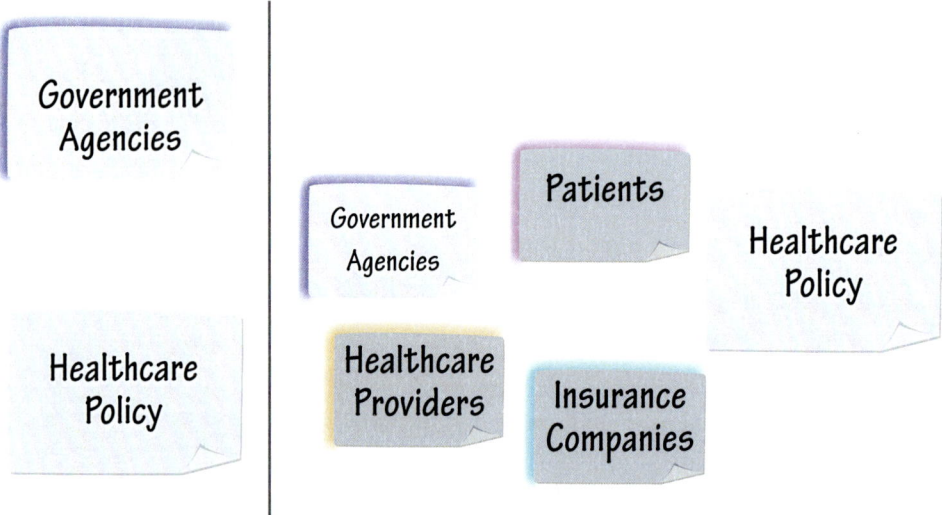

3. Urban Planning:

In urban planning, the P-Circle encompasses the perspectives of architects, city officials, residents, and environmentalists. Balancing aesthetics, functionality, sustainability, and community needs requires acknowledging all these angles.

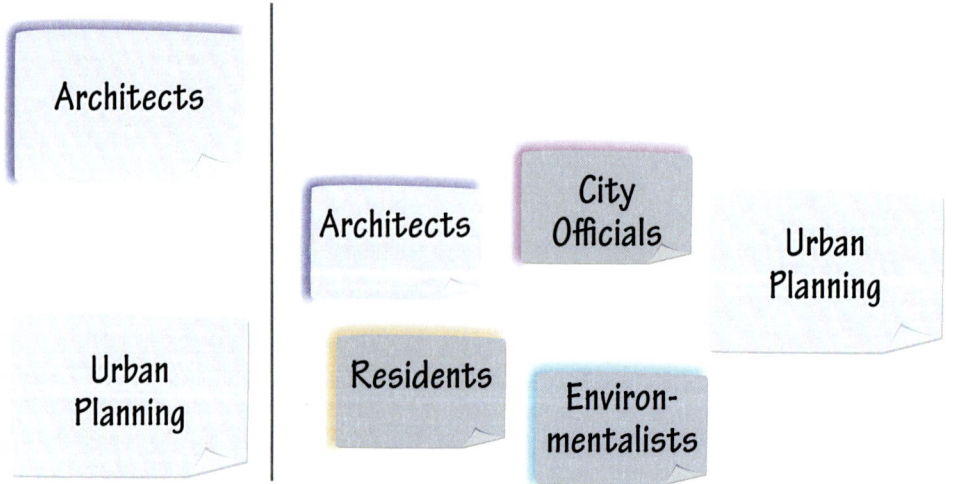

4. Business Ethics:

Business leaders must navigate various ethical perspectives, such as profit-driven, socially responsible, and environmentally sustainable approaches. Understanding these viewpoints helps in making responsible corporate decisions.

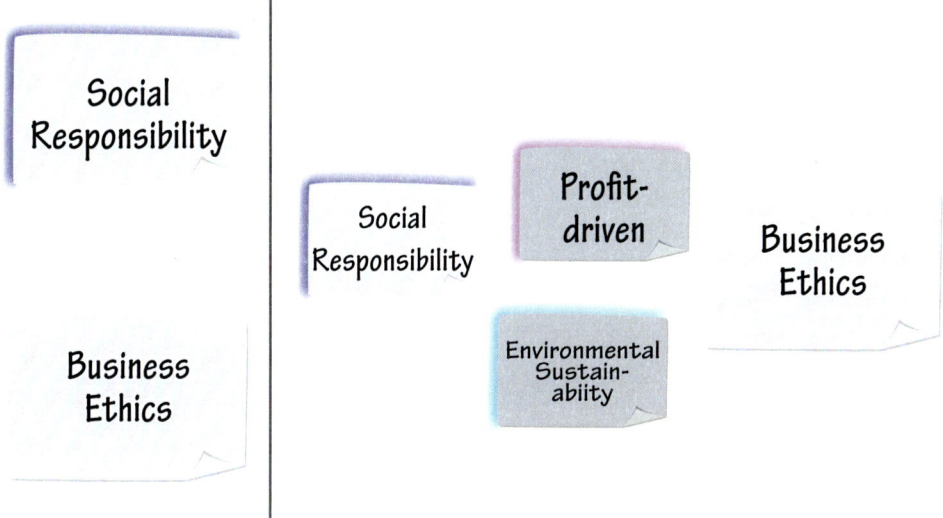

5. Education Reform:

When reforming education systems, policymakers, teachers, parents, and students all have valuable insights to offer. The P-Circle approach ensures that educational reforms consider the needs and expectations of all stakeholders.

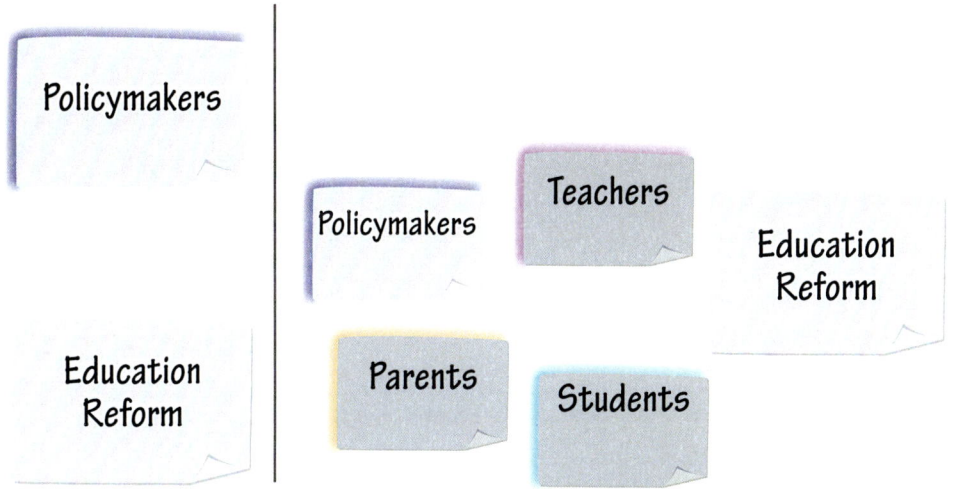

6. International Relations:

In global diplomacy, the P-Circle includes perspectives from diplomats, international organizations, citizens, and grassroots movements. Effective diplomacy requires acknowledging the diverse interests and concerns of these groups.

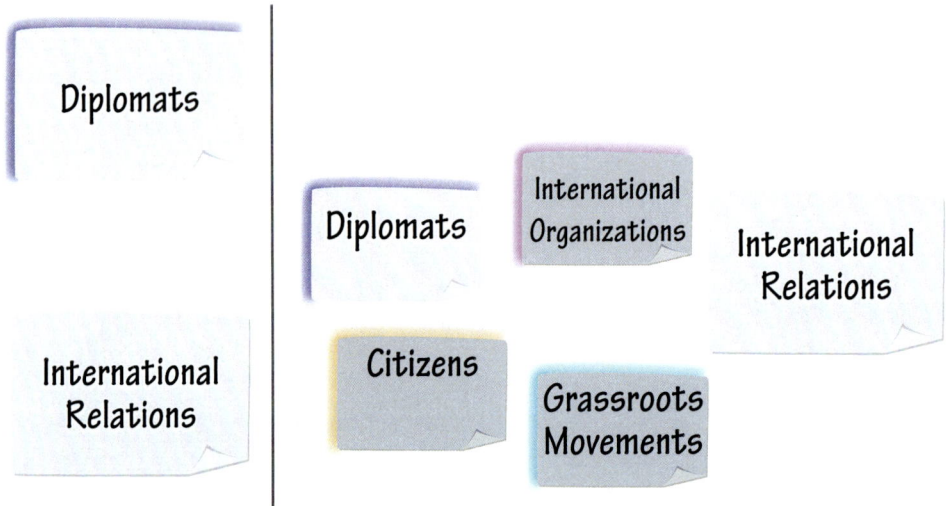

7. Art and Critique:

Art critics, artists, collectors, and gallery owners all bring unique viewpoints to the world of art. The P-Circle allows for a richer appreciation of artistic expression and a deeper understanding of its impact on society.

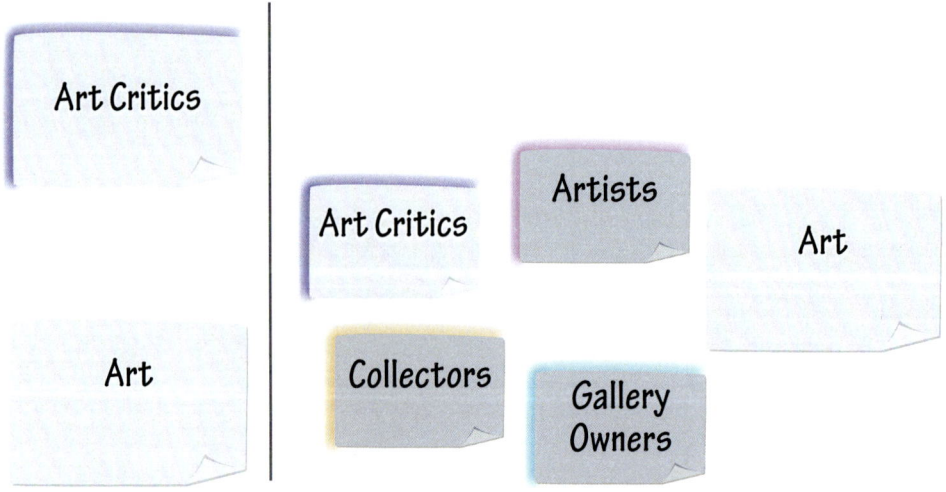

8. Technology Innovation:

In the tech industry, the P-Circle involves the perspectives of engineers, designers, consumers, and regulators. Considering these viewpoints ensures that technological innovations align with societal needs and values.

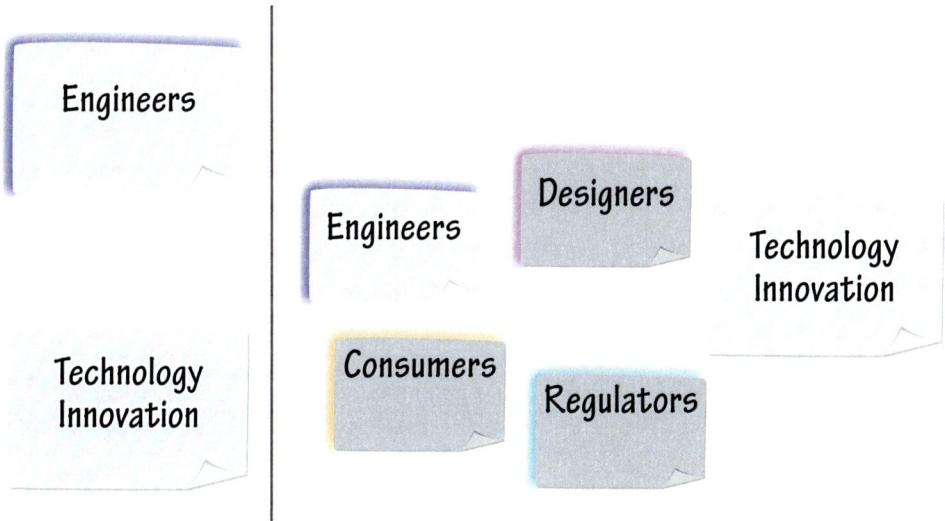

9. Social Justice:

Addressing social justice issues requires acknowledging perspectives from marginalized communities, activists, policymakers, and the broader public. The P-Circle helps build inclusive and equitable solutions.

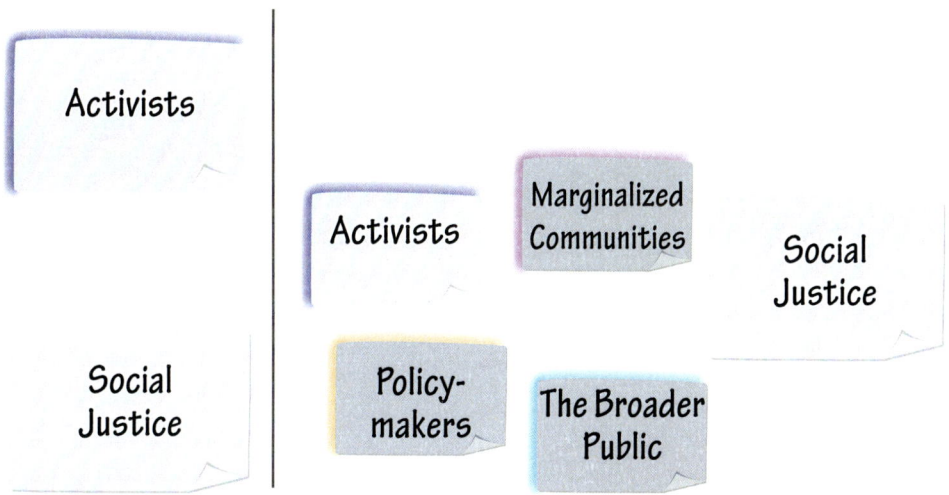

10. Personal Growth:

On an individual level, the P-Circle encourages self-reflection by considering our own perspectives as well as those of our friends, mentors, and diverse sources of inspiration. This approach helps us develop a well-rounded outlook on life and personal growth.

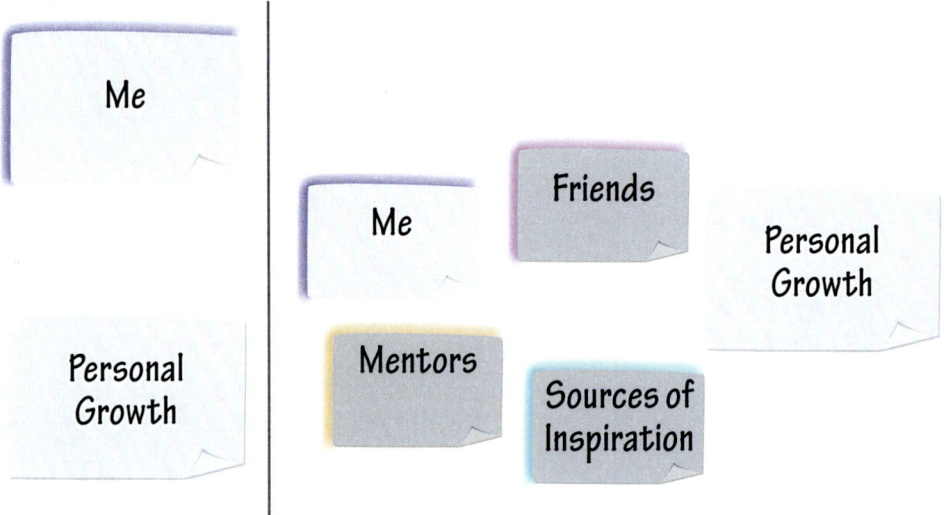

P-Circle: Examples of some popular conceptual perspectives

Economic
Technological
Historical
Social
Health & Safety
Political
Emotional
Moral/Ethical
Security
Ecological
Cultural
Legal
Organizational

These examples illustrate the breadth of perspectives that can be integrated into the P-Circle, ranging from human viewpoints to broader conceptual lenses.

The Limited View: A Cautionary Tale Not to Overlook the P-Circle Move in Life and Work

P-Circle Move - Helps users to explore how any thing could be seen as a different view from numerous points (thus creating points-of-view). It does this by encouraging users to conceptually draw a circle of points around any thing (the view). Each point in the circle can be any thing or concept: a person, group, or even an abstract idea. It helps people to see that things can change depending on how you look at them. It is fundamentally about manipulating the point-view Perspectives (P) pattern of DSRP.

Laura, a dedicated HR manager at a tech company, was tasked with implementing a new performance review system. She aimed to create a process that was fair, transparent, and motivating for the employees. In her personal life, she was planning a surprise birthday party for her husband, wanting to make it a memorable event for him and their friends.

In both her professional project and personal event planning, Laura focused on her own perspective. She designed the performance review system based on what she believed was the best approach, without seeking input from other stakeholders. Similarly, for the birthday party, she planned activities and a guest list based on her own understanding of her husband's preferences.

However, as the performance review system was rolled out and the party date approached, Laura encountered challenges. Employees expressed concerns about the new review process, feeling that it didn't adequately address their needs or concerns. At home, some of the invited guests hinted that the planned activities might not align with her husband's interests.

Laura realized that she had neglected the P-Circle move, failing to consider multiple perspectives in both her professional and personal decisions. Determined to rectify the situation, she decided to apply the P-Circle move to gain a broader understanding.

For the performance review system, Laura organized a series of focus groups with employees from different departments, levels, and backgrounds. She encircled the topic with diverse viewpoints, creating a map to visualize the different perspectives:

Employee

Manager   Peer

System

This map helped Laura see that the System needed to incorporate feedback from Managers, Peers, and Employees to be truly effective. She adjusted the review process to include more diverse input, which led to increased acceptance and satisfaction among the staff.

For the birthday party, Laura reached out to her husband's close friends and family members to gather insights into his preferences. She created a similar map to encircle the event with multiple points of view:

Friend

Family   Colleague

Party

This approach revealed that her husband would prefer a more intimate gathering with close friends and family, rather than the larger event Laura had initially planned. She adjusted the guest list and activities accordingly, resulting in a celebration that was much more in line with her husband's tastes.

Through these experiences, Laura learned the importance of the P-Circle move in both her professional and personal life. She realized that by encircling a topic with multiple perspectives, she could make more informed and effective decisions. From that point on, she committed to always considering diverse viewpoints before finalizing any plans or projects.

Practice

 Choose a topic—anything from a family decision to a global issue—and draw a simple circle. In the center, write the topic. Around it, write down the different perspectives people might have: a child, a neighbor, a rival, an expert, a stranger, your future self. Then step into each one. What do they see? What matters to them? Try this mentally while scrolling your feed or listening to someone vent. With time, you'll find yourself instinctively shifting into different points of view—unlocking empathy, insight, and creativity on the fly. Remember: The goal is not perfection—it's practice. Burn the neurons and they'll be there when you need them.

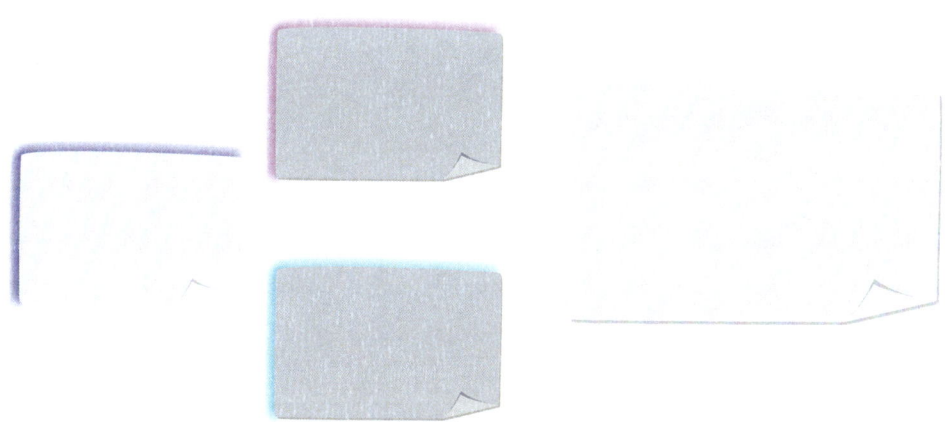

Chapter 13: The Power of Connecting the Dots

Let's explore how mastering this ability can transform the way we think, act, and shape the world around us. The pace of change is accelerating, and information floods our daily lives. But information alone is not knowledge, and complexity without clarity leads to confusion. What sets the best thinkers apart is their ability to see patterns, recognize relationships, and simplify complexity into actionable insight. This is what mental fitness is all about.

Throughout this book, you've learned how to strengthen your thinking using five simple moves—distinguishing ideas clearly, seeing systems within systems, identifying relationships, shifting perspectives, and simplifying the seemingly overwhelming. These moves are the mental equivalent of training your body for endurance, agility, and strength. Just like a physically fit body can adapt to challenges, a mentally fit mind can navigate uncertainty, make better decisions, and uncover solutions that others miss.

Your thoughts shape your actions, and your actions shape the world around you. Every decision, every interaction, every moment of insight has the potential to create a ripple effect that extends far beyond yourself. Whether you're guiding a child's learning, leading a team, solving a scientific problem, designing a product, or making sense of personal challenges, your ability to think clearly defines your impact. Mental fitness is not just about personal growth—it's about making a difference in the world.

The best thinkers are not those with the most information, but those who know how to connect it. You now have the tools to go beyond passive knowledge absorption and into active meaning-making—to take the flood of ideas, concepts, and challenges around you and weave them into clarity, insight, and action. The greatest breakthroughs—whether in science, business, leadership, or life—come not from making things more complicated, but from finding the simple, essential truths hidden within complexity. The mental moves you've learned in this book help you cut through the noise, break big challenges into manageable parts, and see structure where others see chaos.

Instead of feeling paralyzed by complexity, you now have a framework for thinking that allows you to break things down, analyze them, and rebuild them in a way that makes sense. You are no longer at the mercy of overwhelming problems—you have the power to shape, refine, and act with precision.

Like physical fitness, mental fitness is a lifelong journey. The more you practice, the stronger and faster your thinking becomes. These five simple moves aren't a one-time fix—they are a way of thinking that will continue to sharpen your mind and deepen your understanding for years to come. So, where do you go from here? You keep training. You keep applying these moves in your work, your relationships, and your daily decision-making. You keep looking for the hidden patterns and the deeper connections. You keep seeing the bigger picture while mastering the details.

Because in a world that is constantly changing, the ability to connect the dots is the ultimate competitive advantage.

This is your moment to connect the dots. To see complexity as an opportunity, not a barrier. To take control of your thinking and shape a future where you thrive. Get smart, stay sharp, and get results. Your future self—and the world—will thank you for it. Let's be fit for all of life. The dots are there—now it's time to connect them.

Chapter 14: Why Smart People Miss the Obvious

"Dad, let's keep zooming in!" My 4-year-old said it like it was the most obvious thing in the world.

It was summer. I was at my home desk. Bug testing a new piece of software I designed. Cognitive mapping—mapping the mind. My son Carter was four and he was squirming on my lap like an octopus with too many appendages. I needed to find a way to continue testing the software and occupy my son's brain tentacles. The keyboard was too hard to handle with him in my lap so typing words was not an option. But the mouse was possible as I bounced hom on my knee, held him with one arm and moused with the other. Debugging required trying to break the software by clicking in various ways. So I showed Carter one of the cognitive moves—the ability to zoom in by creating parts and parts of parts and so on. He was excited to see its limits and loved repetition so he said, daddy let's keep zooming in and zooming in. We did, down to 37 levels, much farther than most cognitive mapping applications would ever need to go!

Then I showed him how to relate one node to another with connecting lines. He immediately made it a game and said let's try to connect everything to everything else. We connected several dozen nodes and when we ran out we added more and connected those to all the others. The activity went on like this for some time. And then it ended. His mother returned home and he raced off to another part of the house. I went back to bug finding.

But then I noticed something remarkable. He kept talking about it. He used it in conversation. I saw him doing it. He'd say, "Dad, let's zoom into that!" Or "Dad, let's connect those things." These were cognitive patterns I was having a hard time getting my Ivy League doctoral students to see and here was this five year old doing the moves after one sit down! I realized that not being able to use the keyboard—a limitation of having an octopus on my lap—made it so we focused entirely on cognitive structures divorced from the information content we might have typed into these shapes. Yet, my young boy somehow picked up and utilized ideas that were challenging my doctoral students.

Here's the secret: We practiced how to think, not what to think. The thing is, the informational world—is just a tiny tip of the iceberg floating at the surface. It's the world you're familiar with from 12 to 20 years of indoctrinated education and schooling, but there's much, much more beneath the surface. A much larger part of the iceberg is the organizational world—a world of how information is organized. And it is much, much more important to understand in order to be ready, adaptive, and capable of handling whatever life throws at you. Information drives what to think, and it's mostly free and readily available on the internet and in AI. Organization is HOW to think, and it's the crux of being adaptable, ready, skilled, and mentally fit. And that's exactly what you're going to do for yourself when you SEE the underlying structure of your thoughts.

Meet the CEO who outmaneuvered competitors, the teacher who transformed classrooms, and the parent who rewired family dynamics—all using the 5 Moves.Their secret? Mental fitness workouts that make clarity, adaptability, and problem-solving second nature.The 5 Moves aren't magic—they're muscle memory for your brain. Keep practicing, keep flexing, and watch your mental strength skyrocket.

Rethinking Smart

In our journey to redefine what it means to be smart, we've uncovered a profound truth: Smart is no longer about possessing information. Instead, it's about the ability to organize—DSRP—information to adapt to reality. This concept takes on even greater significance when we consider the research that reveals the importance of metacognition, or insights into our own thoughts. As it turns out, metacognition is the key to high achievement in all domains, whether we're talking about analytical intelligence, emotional intelligence, or any other form of intelligence.

One intriguing finding suggests that if you want to develop emotional intelligence, you'd be better off training in metacognition than specifically targeting emotional intelligence itself. It underscores the notion that metacognition is a foundational skill that underpins various facets of intelligence and competence. This insight resonates strongly with the World Economic Forum's list of 21st Century Skills, which highlights the capabilities most required for the jobs of the future. Among these skills are analytical thinking and innovation, creativity and originality, emotional intelligence, critical thinking, complex problem solving, and systems analysis and evaluation.

However, it's essential to recognize that when we talk about these skills, we're focusing on outputs or outcomes. We're looking at the results of cognitive processes. To truly cultivate these skills, we must consider the inputs—the mental processes that enable us to think critically, solve complex problems, and evaluate systems effectively. Enter DSRP—Distinctions, Systems, Relationships, and Perspectives. These are the fundamental inputs that empower us to organize information, make meaningful distinctions, identify systems at play, understand relationships, and embrace diverse perspectives. DSRP is the cognitive toolkit that enables us to develop the very skills that the 21st century demands.

So, when we ponder the future of intelligence and the skills required for success, remember that it all starts with how we think. We're not just talking about the outcomes; we're focusing on the inputs that shape our cognitive prowess. DSRP is the key that unlocks the door to analytical thinking, emotional intelligence, critical problem solving, and the multitude of skills essential for thriving in the complex and ever-evolving world of tomorrow.

The future belongs to those who can think clearly, adapt swiftly, and solve problems with precision. Intelligence isn't just about what we know—it's about how we process, structure, and apply information to make sense of an ever-changing world. DSRP provides the foundation for developing these essential cognitive skills, from analytical thinking to emotional intelligence and critical problem-solving. But understanding how we think is only the beginning. The real power lies in connecting the dots—taking fragmented pieces of information and weaving them into meaningful, actionable insights. In a world where complexity is increasing at an unprecedented rate, the ability to see relationships, recognize patterns, and make sense of uncertainty is no longer optional—it's a survival skill.

You've made it this far. That says something.

Most people don't finish things—books, workouts, goals, conversations. You did. That means you're already practicing the mental fitness required to go deeper.

But now we flip the script.

Because this book? It's not the end of anything. It's the beginning.

It's the warm-up before the real training. The map before the trek. The moment you stop reading and start doing. This is where your journey into clarity, insight, and change *really* begins. Because knowing DSRP isn't the goal. *Doing* DSRP is.

Mental fitness isn't built by having the tools. It's built by using them. Repetition. Application. Awareness. Practice. That's how we wire the brain for adaptability, creativity, resilience, and connection.

You already have everything you need:

- Four universal patterns.
- Eight elemental structures.
- Three deep dynamics.
- Six simple moves.

Now comes the *daily reps*. The way you begin to see your child's behavior not just as a problem—but as a system. The way you respond to an argument with a question instead of a defense. The way you wake up and notice the patterns, the dots, the relationships, the perspectives—in your thoughts, your work, your life.

The world isn't waiting for perfect people. It's waiting for prepared ones.

We don't need more pundits or platforms or pundit platforms. We need thinkers. Quiet warriors of cognition who don't just react—but reflect. Who connect the dots and help others see how everything—and everyone—is interconnected.

You don't have to become someone else to do this work. You just have to become more *you*. A more structured version of yourself. More aware. More grounded. More resilient. More adaptive. A little clearer each day.

If you ever doubt whether it's working, here's how you'll know:

You'll begin to notice what others miss.
You'll ask better questions.
You'll pause before reacting.
You'll build better teams.
You'll feel less overwhelmed by complexity—and more energized by it.
And you'll find that the smallest changes in how you *see* the world…
…can create the biggest shifts in how you *live* in it.

Mental fitness doesn't make life easier. It makes *you* stronger.

So practice. Not for perfection. But for clarity.

Practice, because complexity isn't going anywhere. But neither is your potential.

Practice, because the dots are already connected in real life..

Practice, because the dots aren't going to connect themselves.

And practice, because the future belongs to those who can adapt and think it into being.

See more. Do more. Be more.

Connect the dots.

Appendix 1

Pattern & Elements	DSRP Findings after <1 intervention	Mental Fintness Move(s)	Moves Findings after <1 intervention
Distinction (D) = identity (i) ↔ other (o) D =i ↔o	+43% increase in word use, +41% increase in character complexity (IRR = 1.43 and 1.41, p < .001)	**Is/Is Not List Move**	5.51x or 551% increase in problem solving, higher order thinking and emotional intelligence (p < 0.01)
Systems (S) = part (p) ↔ whole (w) S = p ↔ w	+13.2% word use, +41.6% unique words, +49.2% increase in character complexity of unique words (p < 0.001 for number of concepts)	**Zoom In Move** **Zoom Out Move**	2.66x or 266% increase in problem solving, higher order thinking and emotional intelligence (p < 0.01)
Relationships (R) = action (a) ↔ reaction (r) R = a ↔ r	+15.5% in word use (p < .001), richer relational language and concept depth	**Part Party! Move**	2.47x or 247% increase in problem solving, higher order thinking and emotional intelligence (p < 0.01)
		RDS Barbell Move	5.08x or 508% increase in problem solving, higher order thinking and emotional intelligence (p < 0.01)
Perspectives (P) = view (v) ↔ point ($\dot{p}$) P = v ↔ $\dot{p}$	+16.5% increase in word use, significant increase in varied perspectives and narrative complexity (p = 0.002 for concepts; p = 0.013 for characters)	**Perspective Circle Move (P-Circle).**	4.47x or 447% increase in problem solving, higher order thinking and emotional intelligence (p < 0.01)